THE RES[illegible] of CANADA JOKE BOOK

Introduction

Canada is a funny place. We are a nation of diverse peoples and places, and the one thing that unites us all (besides hockey) is our sense of humour.

It is an aspect of our nature that grew out of necessity, having to live in a country where it can be –40°C in winter and 35°C in summer. To tolerate our climate, we Canadians had to develop a sense of humour. It was necessary for survival. Huddled around a small fire in the middle of winter, the early settlers told jokes to keep themselves from killing each other. But our humour is more than simple weather jokes. As our nation has grown and expanded, and as we've gone through trials and tribulations together, we have carved out a unique way of looking at the world. If jokes are a reflection of a society, then Canadians are truly a strange lot. I have gathered a vast sample of regional and national jokes about what it means to be Canadian and how we have come to see each other. These jokes are not meant to divide but to unite us with laughter (though Québec might get offended and want to leave this book). In them, you will find all types of Canadians and jokes about what it means to be Canadian, from the standard (and expected) Newfie jokes, to Québec political jokes, political corruption in Ottawa, rednecks from Alberta, Vancouver hippies and many more. I have tried to include all kinds of Canadians and their various stereotypes to ensure that no one is left out and that we come together in laughter and self-deprecation.

Chapter One
What It Means to Be Canadian

Only in Canada

Only in Canada...are there handicap parking spaces in front of a skating rink.

Only in Canada...do we leave cars worth thousands of dollars in the driveway and put our useless junk in the garage.

> In Canada we have two seasons...six months of winter and six months of poor hockey weather.

Only in Canada...can a pizza get to your house faster than an ambulance.

Only in Canada...do drugstores make the sick walk all the way to the back of the store to get their prescriptions while healthy people can buy cigarettes at the front.

Only in Canada...do we buy hot dogs in packages of 12 and buns in packages of eight.

Only in Canada...do they have drive-up ATM machines with Braille lettering.

You know you've had too much to drink when you look at advertisement that reads "Drink Canada Dry" and take it as a challenge.

The Canadian Temperature Conversion Chart

- 50°F (10°C)

  Californians shiver uncontrollably. Canadians plant gardens.

- 35°F (1.6°C)

  Italian cars won't start. Canadians drive with the windows down.

- 32°F (0°C)

  American water freezes. Canadian water gets thicker.

- 0°F (–17.9°C)

  New York City landlords finally turn on the heat. Canadians have the last cookout of the season.

- –60°F (–51°C)

  Mount St. Helens freezes. Canadian Girl Guides sell cookies door-to-door.

- –100°F (–73°C)

  Santa Claus abandons the North Pole. Canadians pull down their earflaps.

- –173°F (–114°C)

  Ethyl alcohol freezes. Canadians get frustrated when they can't thaw the keg.

- –460°F (–273°C)

  Absolute zero; all atomic motion stops. Canadians start saying, "Cold, eh?"

- –500°F (–295°C)

  Hell freezes over. The Toronto Maple Leafs win the Stanley Cup.

Through Europe

Three men are travelling in Europe and happen to meet at a bar in London. One man is from England, one from France and one from Canada. They get acquainted and start talking about the problems they have with their wives.

The guy from England says, "I told my wife in no uncertain terms that from now on she has to do the cooking. Well, the first day after I told her, I saw nothing. The second day, I saw nothing. But on the third day when I came home from work, the table was set and a wonderful dinner was prepared with wine and even dessert."

Then the man from France speaks up. "I sat my wife down and told her that from now on she has to do all the shopping and cleaning. The first day, I saw nothing. The second day, I saw nothing. But on the third day when I came home, the whole house was spotless, and in the pantry the shelves were filled with groceries."

"Canada has never been a melting-pot; more like a tossed salad."

–Arnold Edinborough

The fellow from Canada is married to an enlightened woman from the prairies. He sits up straight on the bar stool, pushes out his chest and says, "I gave my wife a stern look and told her that from now on she has to do the cooking, shopping and housecleaning. Well, the first day, I saw nothing. The second day, I still saw nothing. But on the third day, I could see a little bit out of my left eye...."

Perceptions of Canada

When Vancouver won the chance to host the 2010 Winter Olympics, people from around the world started asking questions about Canada. The questions were posted on a website, and a Canadian with a wicked dry sense of humour answered back:

Q: I have never seen it warm on Canadian TV, so how do the plants grow? (England)

A: We import all plants fully grown and then just sit around and watch them die.

> "In any world menu, Canada must be considered the vichyssoise of nations; it's cold, half-French and difficult to stir."
>
> –Stuart Keate

Q: Will I be able to see polar bears in the street? (USA)

A: Depends on how much you've been drinking.

Q: I want to walk from Vancouver to Toronto. Can I follow the railroad tracks? (Sweden)

A: Sure, it's only 4000 miles. Take lots of water.

Q: Is it safe to run around in the bushes in Canada? (Sweden)

A: So it's true what they say about Swedes.

Q: Are there any ATMs (cash machines) in Canada? Can you send me a list of them in Toronto, Vancouver, Edmonton and Halifax? (England)

A: What, did your last slave die?

Q: Can you give me some information about hippo racing in Canada? (USA)

A: A-fri-ca is the big triangle-shaped continent south of Europe. Ca-na-da is that big country to your north...nevermind. Sure, the hippo racing is every Tuesday night in Calgary. Come naked.

Q: Which direction is north in Canada? (USA)

A: Face south and then turn 180 degrees. Contact us when you get here and we'll send the rest of the directions.

Q: Can I bring cutlery into Canada? (England)

A: Why? Just use your fingers like we do.

Q: Do you have perfume in Canada? (Germany)

A: No, WE don't stink.

Q: I have developed a new product that is the fountain of youth. Where can I sell it in Canada? (USA)

A: Anywhere significant numbers of Americans gather.

Q: How do you stop bacon from curling in the frying pan?

A: Take away its brooms.

Q: Can you tell me the regions in British Columbia where the female population is smaller than the male population? (Italy)

A: Yes, gay nightclubs.

Q: Do you celebrate Thanksgiving in Canada? (USA)

A: Only at Thanksgiving.

Q: Are there supermarkets in Toronto and is milk available all year round? (Germany)

A: No, we are a peaceful civilization of vegan hunter/gathers. Milk is illegal.

Q: I have a question about a famous animal in Canada, but I forget its name. It's a kind of big horse with horns. (USA)

A: It's called a moose. They are tall and very violent, eating the brains of anyone walking close to them. You can scare them off by spraying yourself with human urine before you go out walking.

Q: Will I be able to speak English most places I go? (USA)

A: Yes, but you will have to learn it first.

How to Live

The Japanese eat very little fat and suffer fewer heart attacks than the British or Canadians.

On the other hand, the French eat a lot of fat and also suffer fewer heart attacks than the British or Canadians.

Q: How do you kiss a hockey player?

A: Puck-er up.

The Japanese drink very little red wine and suffer fewer heart attacks than the British or Canadians.

The Italians drink excessive amounts of red wine and also suffer fewer heart attacks than the British or Canadians.

Conclusion: Eat and drink what you like. It's speaking English that kills you.

The Many Uses of Eh!

We Canadians have a unique way of conversing. From BC to Newfoundland, there are different accents and uses for words, but two simple letters unite us all: *eh* (pronounced *ay*—just putting this in here in case an American picks up the book, eh!). So, what exactly does it mean? With a few changes in tone and depending on the situation, this one little word can mean a million different things.

> "Canada is the essence of not being. Not English, not American, it is the mathematic of not being. And a subtle flavour. We're more like celery as a flavour."
>
> –Mike Myers

Eh = Something to say just to end a sentence. "So I was going to the grocery store, eh."

Eh? = What did you say?

Eh? = What do you think?

Ehhhh!! = WOW!!

EH!? = What do you mean?

Eh?? = You're joking!!!??

EH!! = Hello!! (you, off in the distance!!!)

Eh? = Habs or Maple Leafs?

Eh! = Sure!!

Eh! Eh! = That puck crossed the line!

F*ckin' eh! = It's cold out here! Or, yeah, that's awesome!

Holy f*ckin' eh! = A Canadian team won the Cup!

Eh? = What you say when you realize you have no money to pay for something.

Eh...c'mon, eh? = How you ask to be allowed to pay for it next time.

Eh...wanna, eh? = Let's fool around.

EHHHHHHH = sounds coming from the car.

Hey...um...er, eh... = I'm pregnant!

EH????????? = How did that happen?

Bank President

A little old lady goes into the Bank of Canada carrying a bag of money. She insists that she must speak with the president of the bank to open a savings account because, "It's a lot of money!"

After much humming and hawing, the bank staff finally usher her into the president's office (the customer is always right!). The bank president then asks her how much she would like to deposit.

She replies, "One hundred and sixty-five thousand dollars!" and dumps the cash out of her bag onto his desk.

Of course, the president is curious as to how she came by all this cash, so he says to her, "Ma'am, I'm surprised you're carrying so much cash around. Where did you get this money?"

> "Canadians are an ambivalent lot–one minute they want to be peacekeepers, next minute they punch the hell out of each other on the ice rink."
>
> –Ken Wiwa

The old lady replies, "I make bets."

"Bets?" the president asks. "What kind of bets?"

The old woman says, "Well, for example, I'll bet you $25,000 that your balls are square."

"Ha!" laughs the president. "That's a stupid bet. You can never win that kind of bet!"

The old lady challenges, "So, would you like to take my bet?"

"Sure," says the president. "I'll bet $25,000 that my balls are not square!"

The little old lady says, "Okay, but because there is a lot of money involved, may I bring my lawyer with me tomorrow at 10:00 AM as a witness?"

"Sure!" replies the confident president.

That night, the president is nervous about the bet and spends a long time in front of the mirror studying his balls, turning from side to side, again and again. He thoroughly checks them out until he is sure that there is absolutely no way his balls are square and that he will win the bet.

The next morning, at precisely 10:00 AM, the little old lady appears with her lawyer at the president's office. She introduces the lawyer to the president and repeats the bet: "Twenty-five thousand dollars says the president's balls are square!"

The president agrees with the bet again, and the old lady asks him to drop his pants so they can all see. The president complies. The little old lady peers closely at his balls.

"Can I feel them?" she asks.

"Well, okay," says the president. "There's a lot of money at stake, so I guess you should be absolutely sure." Just then, he notices that her lawyer is quietly banging his head against the wall. The president asks the old lady, "What the hell's the matter with your lawyer?"

She replies, "Nothing, except I bet him $100,000 that at 10:00 AM today, I'd have the Bank of Canada's president's balls in my hand."

Ten Things You Should Never Say to a Canadian

10. "Do you know Bob from Calgary?"
9. "I would like to visit your nation's capital. Toronto, right?"
8. "What's a Tim Hortons?"
7. "Who is Wayne Gretzky?"
6. "Thank you for Nickelback. I love them!"
5. "Private health care is the way to go."
4. "Basketball is better than hockey!"
3. "I bet you love Celine Dion."
2. "So, like, do you, like, ride polar bears and live in igloos?"
1. "Your beer sucks!"

When the loonie first came out, there was almost a political crisis in Ottawa. Politicians spent hours in their offices trying to take off the foil and get to the chocolate inside.

Out of Luck

A Québecois, a Newfie and a Toronto asshole are at the beach. Suddenly, they spy a beautiful mermaid sunning herself in a shoal.

The Québecois walks up to her with desire in his eyes and says, "Beautiful mermaid, have you ever been keesed?"

The mermaid says, "No, I haven't."

I was born in Canada. Which part? All of me.

So the Québecois says, "Zen I weel show you." And he kisses the mermaid passionately for half an hour.

Then the Newfie speaks up. "Hey der, mermaid, have you ever been fondled?"

The mermaid says, "No."

So the Newfie says, "Then I will-a show you." And the Newfie passionately fondles the mermaid for half an hour.

Then the asshole speaks. "Beautiful mermaid, have ya ever been skrooed?"

The mermaid says, "No, I haven't."

To this, the asshole replies, "Well, ya have now. The tide went out an hour ago!"

A Canadian tourist goes into a restaurant in Spain and orders the house special. When his dinner arrives, he asks the waiter what it is.

"These, *señor,*" replies the waiter in broken English, "are the *cojones,* how you say, the testicles, of the bull killed in the ring today."

The tourist swallows hard but decides to taste the dish, and he thinks it is delicious. So he comes back the next evening and orders the same item. When it is served, he says to the waiter, "These *cojones,* or whatever you call them, are much smaller than the ones I had last night."

"Si, *señor,*" replies the waiter. "You see...the bull, he does not always lose."

The Good Life

A Canadian businessman is on the pier of a small coastal Mexican village when a boat with just one fisherman docks. Inside the small boat are several large yellowfin tuna. The Canadian compliments the Mexican on the quality of his fish and asks how long it took to catch them. The Mexican replies, "Only a little while."

The Canadian then asks the fisherman why he didn't stay out longer and catch more fish. The Mexican answers that he has enough to meet his family's immediate needs.

So the Canadian asks, "But what do you do with the rest of your time?"

The Mexican fisherman says, "I sleep late, fish a little, play with my children, take siesta with my wife, Maria, and stroll into the village each evening where I sip wine and play guitar with my *amigos*. I have a full and busy life, *señor*."

The Canadian scoffs, "I have an MBA and can help you. You should spend more time fishing and with the proceeds buy a bigger boat. With the proceeds from the bigger boat, you could buy several boats. Eventually you could have a fleet of fishing boats. Instead of selling your catch to a middleman, you could sell directly to the processor, eventually opening your own cannery. You would control the product, processing and distribution. You would have to leave this small coastal fishing village and move to Mexico City and eventually New York City, where you would run your expanding enterprise."

The Mexican fisherman asks, "But *señor*, how long will this all take?"

To which the Canadian replies, "About 15 to 20 years."

"But what then, *señor?*"

The Canadian laughs and says, "That's the best part. When the time is right, you could sell your company stock to the public and become very rich. You would make millions!"

"Millions, *señor?* Then what?"

The Canadian says, "Then you would retire, move to a small coastal fishing village where you would sleep late, fish a little, play with your kids, take siesta with your wife and stroll to the village in the evenings, where you could sip wine and play your guitar with your amigos."

German scientists dig 50 metres underground and discover small pieces of copper. After studying these pieces for a long time, Germany announces that 25,000 years ago the ancient Germans had a nationwide telephone network.

Naturally, the British government is not that easily impressed. They order their own scientists to dig even deeper. One hundred metres down, they find small pieces of glass, and they soon announce that the ancient Brits already had a nationwide fibre net 35,000 years ago.

Canadian scientists are outraged. They dig 50, 100 and 200 metres underground but find absolutely nothing, so they conclude that 55,000 years ago the ancient people of North America had cell phones.

Bar Games

A local bar is so sure that its bartender is the strongest man around that they offer a standing $1000 bet. The bartender squeezes a lemon until all the juice runs into a glass and then hands the lemon to a patron. Anyone who can squeeze out one more drop of juice wins the money.

Many people try over time—weight-lifters, longshoremen, etc.—but nobody can do it.

One day, a scrawny little man wearing thick glasses and a polyester suit comes into the bar and says in a tiny, squeaky voice, "I'd like to try the bet."

Once the laughter dies down, the bartender grabs a lemon and squeezes away. He then hands the wrinkled remains of the rind to the little man.

The crowd's snickering turns to stunned silence as the man clenches his fist around the lemon and squeezes six drops into the glass.

As the crowd cheers, the bartender pays the $1000 and asks the little man, "What do you do for a living? Are you a lumberjack, a weight-lifter or what?"

The scrawny little man replies, "I work for the Canada Revenue Agency."

Not All Polite

A World War II Canadian soldier has been on the front lines in Europe for three months when he is finally given a week of R&R. He catches a supply boat to a supply base in the south of England, and then catches a train to London. The train is extremely crowded and he cannot find a seat. He is dead on his feet and walks the length of the train looking for a place to sit down.

Finally, he finds a compartment with seats facing each other; there is room for two people on each seat. On one side sits an older, proper-looking British lady with a small dog sitting in the empty seat beside her.

"Could I please sit in that seat?" the soldier asks.

The lady is insulted. "You Canadians are so rude," she says. "Can't you see my dog is sitting there?"

The man continues to walk through the train but still cannot find a seat. He ends up back at the same place.

"Lady, I love dogs—have a couple at home—and I would be glad to hold your dog if I can sit down," he says.

The lady replies, "You Canadians are not only rude, you are arrogant."

He leans against the wall for a time but is so tired he finally says, "Lady, I've been on the front lines in Europe for three months with no decent rest for all that time. Could I please sit there and hold your dog?"

The lady replies, "You Canadians are not only rude and arrogant, you are also obnoxious."

With that comment, the soldier calmly steps in, picks up the dog, throws it out the window and sits down. The lady is speechless.

An older, neatly dressed Englishman sitting in the seat across from the soldier speaks up. "Young man, I do not know if all Canadians fit the lady's description of you or not. But I do know that you Canadians do a lot of things wrong. You drive on the wrong side of the road, you hold your fork with the wrong hand and now you have just thrown the wrong bitch out of the window."

Canadian Fairy Tale

Once upon a time, a prince asked a princess, "Will you marry me?"

She said, "No."

...And the guy lived happily ever after and went fishing and hunting and drank beer all day every day for the rest of his life.

THE END

A Russian Favour

Russian President Vladimir Putin calls Prime Minister Stephen Harper with an emergency. "Our largest condom factory has exploded!" the Russian president cries. "It's my people's favourite form of birth control. This is a true disaster!"

"Mr. Putin, the Canadian people would be happy to do anything within our power to help you," replies the Prime Minister.

"I do need your help," says Putin. "Could you possibly send 1,000,000 condoms ASAP to tide us over?"

"Why certainly! I'll get right on it," says Harper.

"Oh, and one more small favour, please?" says Putin.

"Yes?"

"Could the condoms be red and at least 25 centimetres long and 10 centimetres in diameter?" says Putin.

"No problem," replies the Prime Minister.

Putin hangs up and starts laughing with his aides about how those stupid Canadians will fall for anything.

Harper hangs up and calls the president of a condom company. "I need a favour. You've got to send 1,000,000 condoms over to Russia right away."

"Consider it done," says the president of the condom company.

"Great! Now listen, they have to be red, 25 centimetres long and 10 centimetres wide."

"Easily done. Anything else?"

"Yeah," says the Prime Minister. "Print 'MADE IN CANADA, SIZE: SMALL' on each one."

Q: *How many people work at Canada Post?*

A: *Oh, about half of them.*

A team of Canadian archaeologists excavating in Israel come upon a cave. Written on the wall of the cave are the following symbols in order of appearance:

1. a woman
2. a donkey
3. a shovel
4. a fish
5. a Star of David

The archaeologists decide their unique find is at least 3000 years old. They chop out the piece of stone and bring it to a museum where archaeologists from all over the world come to study the ancient symbols. After months of conferences, they hold a huge meeting to discuss the meaning of the markings.

The president of their society stands up, points at the first drawing and says, "This looks like a woman. We can judge that this race was family oriented and held women in high esteem. You can also tell they were intelligent because the next symbol resembles a donkey, so they were smart enough to have animals help them till the soil. The next drawing looks like a shovel of some sort, which indicates they had tools. Even further proof of their high intelligence is the fish symbol, which means that they knew they could also turn to the sea for food. The last symbol appears to be the Star of David, meaning they were evidently Hebrews."

The audience applauds enthusiastically, and the president smiles and says, "I'm glad to see that you are all in full agreement with our interpretations."

Suddenly a little old man stands up in the back of the room and says, "I object to every word. The meaning of the writings is quite simple. You've been 'reading' and 'interpreting' these inscriptions from left to right, but everyone knows that the Hebrews would have written from right to left. Now, look again. It says, 'Holy mackerel, dig the ass on that woman!'"

A baby seal walks into a bar. The bartender asks, "What'll you have?"

The seal replies, "Anything but a Canadian Club!"

Beer Trip

The biggest beer producers in the world meet for a conference, and at the end of the day, the presidents of all the beer companies decide to have a drink together at a bar.

The president of Budweiser naturally orders a Bud, the president of Miller orders a Miller, Adolph Coors orders a Coors, and so on down the list.

Then the bartender asks Jeff Molson what he wants to drink, and to everybody's amazement, he orders tea.

"Why don't you order a Molson?" his colleagues ask suspiciously, wondering if they've stumbled onto an embarrassing secret.

"Naaaah," replies Molson. "If you guys aren't going to drink beer, then neither will I."

Taking Care of Business

A Canadian tourist in London finds himself needing to go to the bathroom something terrible. After a long search, he just can't find any public bathrooms to relieve himself, so he goes down one of the side streets to take care of business. Just as he is unzipping, a London police officer shows up.

"Look here, old chap, what are you doing?" the officer asks.

"I'm sorry," the Canadian replies, "but I really gotta go."

"You can't do that here," the officer tells him. "Look, follow me."

The police officer leads him to a beautiful garden with lots of grass, pretty flowers and manicured hedges.

"Here," says the policeman, "whiz away."

The Canadian tourist shrugs, turns, unzips and starts urinating on the flowers. "Ahhh," he says in relief. When he's done, he turns to the officer and says, "This is very nice of you. Is this British courtesy?"

"No," replies the policeman. "It's the French Embassy."

Spit it Out!

A father walks into a restaurant with his young son. He gives the young boy three nickels to play with to keep him occupied.

Suddenly, the boy starts choking, going blue in the face. The father realizes the boy has swallowed the nickels and starts slapping him on the back.

The boy coughs up two of the nickels but keeps choking. Looking at his son, the father panics and starts shouting for help.

An attractive, serious-looking woman in a blue business suit is sitting at a coffee bar reading a newspaper and sipping a cup of coffee. At the sound of the commotion, she looks up, puts her coffee cup down, neatly folds the newspaper and places it on the counter. She gets up from her seat and makes her way, unhurried, across the restaurant.

Reaching the boy, the woman calmly drops his pants, takes hold of the boy's testicles and starts to squeeze and twist, gently at first and then more firmly. After a few seconds, the boy convulses violently and coughs up the last nickel, which the woman deftly catches in her free hand.

Releasing the boy's testicles, the woman hands the nickel to the father and walks back to her seat at the coffee bar without saying a word.

As soon as he is sure that his son has suffered no ill effects, the father rushes over to the woman to thank her, saying, "I've never seen anybody do anything like that before. It was fantastic. Are you a doctor?"

"No," the woman replies. "I'm with the Canada Revenue Agency."

A federal government employee sits in his office and, out of boredom, decides to see what's in his old filing cabinet. He pokes through the contents and comes across an old brass lamp.

"This will look nice on my mantelpiece," he decides and takes it home with him.

While he is polishing the lamp, a genie appears and grants him three wishes.

"I wish for an ice-cold diet cola right now!"

He gets his cola and drinks it. Now that he can think more clearly, he states his second wish.

"I wish to be on an island where beautiful nymphomaniacs reside."

Suddenly he is on an island with gorgeous females eyeing him lustfully. He tells the genie his third and last wish. "I wish I'd never have to work ever again."

POOF! He's back in his government office.

40 SIGNS THAT YOU MAY BE CANADIAN:

40. You stand in "line-ups" at the movie, not lines.
39. You know it's pronounced *Jay Zed* and not *Jay Zee.*
38. You understand the phrase, "Could you please pass me a serviette. I just spilled my poutine."
37. You eat chocolate bars instead of candy bars.
36. You drink pop, not soda.
35. You know what it means to be on pogey.
34. You know that a mickey and two-four mean "Party at the camp, eh!!"
33. You can drink legally while still a teenager.
32. You talk about the weather with strangers and friends alike.

31. You don't know or care about the fuss with Cuba; it's just a cheap place to travel with good cigars and no Americans.
30. When there is a social problem, you turn to your government to fix it instead of telling them to stay out of it.
29. You're not sure if the leader of your nation has EVER had sex and don't want to know if he has.
28. You get milk in bags as well as cartons and plastic jugs.
27. Pike is a type of fish, not some part of a highway.
26. You drive on a highway, not a freeway.
25. If someone asks you to sit on the chesterfield, you know what to do.
24. You know what a Robertson screwdriver is.
23. You have Canadian Tire money in your kitchen drawers.
22. You know that Thrills are something to chew and "taste like soap."
21. You know that Mounties "don't always look like that."
20. You dismiss all beers under 6 percent alcohol content as "for children and the elderly."
19. You know that the Friendly Giant isn't a vegetable product line.
18. You know that Casey and Finnegan are not a Celtic musical group.
17. You participated in "Participaction."

16. You have an Inuit carving by your bedside with the rationale, "What's good enough protection for the Prime Minister is good enough for me."
15. You wonder why there isn't a $5 coin yet.
14. Unlike any international assassin, terrorist or spy in the world, you possess a Canadian passport.
13. You use a red pen on your non-Canadian textbooks and fill in the missing "u"s from labor, honor and color.
12. You know the French equivalents of "free," "prize" and "no sugar added" thanks to your extensive education in bilingual cereal packaging.
11. You are excited whenever an American television show mentions Canada.
10. You make a mental note to talk about it at work the next day.
9. You can do all the hand actions to Sharon, Lois and Bram's "Skin-a-ma-rinky-dinky-doo" opus.
8. You can eat more than one maple sugar candy without feeling nauseated.
7. You were mad when *The Beachcombers* was taken off the air.
6. You know what a toque is.
5. You have some memento of Bob and Doug.
4. You tell all your American friends that Ryan Reynolds and Ryan Gosling are Canadian.
3. You know Toronto is not a province.
2. You never miss *Coach's Corner.*
1. Back bacon and Kraft Dinner are two of your favourite food groups.

A Canadian Is Someone Who...

Drinks Brazilian coffee...from an English teacup...and munches a French pastry...while sitting on his Swedish furniture...having just come home from an Italian movie...in his German car. He picks up his Japanese pen...and writes to his Member of Parliament to complain about the American takeover of the Canadian publishing business.

An American, a Scot and a Canadian are in a terrible car accident. They are taken to the same emergency room, but all three die on the way. Just as the toe tag is about to be put on the American's body, he stirs and opens his eyes. Astonished, the doctors and nurses ask him what happened.

"Well," says the American, "I remember the crash, and then there was a beautiful light, and then the Canadian, the Scot and I were standing at the gates of heaven. St. Peter approached us and said that we were all too young to die, and said that for a donation of $50, we could return to Earth. So, of course, I pulled out my wallet and gave him the $50, and the next thing I knew I was back here."

"That's amazing!" says the one of the doctors. "But what happened to the other two men?"

"Last I saw them," replies the American, "the Scot was haggling over the price, and the Canadian was waiting for the government to pay it."

Journalism

Several years before the Gulf War, a Canadian female journalist writes a story on gender roles in Kuwait. She notes that it is customary for women to walk 3 metres behind their husbands.

After the war, she returns to Kuwait and is pleased to observe that now the men walk 3 metres behind their wives. She approaches a woman at the airport and asks, “What enabled Kuwaiti women to achieve this role reversal?”

The Kuwaiti woman replies, “Land mines.”

Chapter Two
East Coast Swing

It's All Yours

Newfoundland is the only province that does not have a First Nations reserve. The land was happily handed over to the Newfies.

An Ontarian, an Albertan and a Newfie are running from the cops. They dash into an alley and see a pile of sacks, which they decide to hide in. The cops follow them into the alley and kick the bag with the Ontarian in it.

The Ontarian goes, "Meow!"

The cops say, "Ah, it's just a bag full of cats."

They kick the bag with the Albertan in it, and he goes, "Woof!"

The cops think, *Okay, dog in a bag, whatever.*

Then they kick the bag with the Newfie in it, and he goes, "Potato!"

The Burly American

A Newfie, a little man, is sitting at a bar in Toronto when a huge, burly American guy walks in. As he passes the Newfie, he hits him on the neck, knocking him to the floor. The big, burly Yank says,

"That's a karate chop from Korea." The Newfie gets back on his barstool and resumes drinking his beer.

The burly American then gets up to go to the bathroom and, as he walks by the Newfie, hits him on the other side of the neck and knocks him to the floor. "That's a judo chop from Japan," he says.

Did you hear about the war between Newfoundland and Nova Scotia? The Newfies were lobbing hand grenades, and the Nova Scotians were pulling the pins and throwing them back.

The Newfie decides he's had enough and leaves. A half hour later, he comes back and sees the burly American sitting at the bar. He walks up behind him and smacks him on the head, knocking him out.

The Newfie says to the bartender, "When he wakes up, b'y, tell him dat was a frickin' crowbar from Canadian Tire."

A gas station in Halifax is trying to increase its sales, so the owner puts up a sign saying "Free Sex With Fill-Up." Soon, a Newfie pulls in, fills his tank and then asks for his free sex.

The gas attendant tells him pick to a number from 1 to 10, and if he guesses correctly, he will get his free sex.

The Newfie says, "Eight, b'y."

"You were close, sir," the gas attendant says, "but the number was seven. Sorry, no sex this time."

A week later, the same Newfie, along with his buddy, pulls in for a fill-up. Again, he asks for his free sex and again the gas attendant gives him the same story and asks him to guess the correct number.

The Newfie says, "Four, b'y."

"Sorry," the gas attendant says, "it was three. You were close, but no free sex this time."

As they are driving away, the Newfie says to his buddy, "I think that game is rigged, and he doesn't really give away free sex."

The buddy replies, "No, b'y, it ain't rigged. My wife won twice last week."

Newfie and the Fish

A guy sees a Newfie walking down the street carrying a bag of fish.

He walks over to the Newfie and says, "Hey Newfie, I bet I can guess how many fish you have in that bag. If I get it right, will you give me one of them?"

And the Newfie says, "Heck, if you can guess how many fish I have in this bag, I'll give 'em both to you."

A deep thought: Do fish get thirsty?

Smart Guy

A Newfie calls the RCMP. "Hello, is this the RCMP? I'm calling about my neighbour, Billy Bob Smith. He is hiding marijuana in his firewood!"

The next day, the RCMP descend on Billy Bob's house and search the shed where the firewood is kept. They bust open every piece of firewood but find no marijuana. They apologize to Billy Bob and leave. The phone rings at Billy Bob's.

"Hey Billy Bob, did the RCMP come to your house?"

"Yep."

"Did they chop all your firewood?"

"Yep."

"Happy birthday, buddy!"

One Tough Islander

Much to the horror of local residents, Satan suddenly appears on the streets of Corner Brook, Newfoundland, and sends everybody in the town running for their lives, except for one old man who calmly sits on a park bench reading a newspaper. Satan's fury grows as he rages through the town, but the old man barely lifts his head.

> Did you know that Rita McNeil has a tattoo of Canada on her butt? Every time she bends over, Québec separates!

"Aren't you scared of me?" Satan screams at the man.

"Nope," says the old timer.

"Aren't you terrified that I am going to destroy your nice little community?"

"Nope," answers the old man.

Satan's fury grows. "You do know who I am? I am evil incarnate! I am the destroyer of souls! I am your worst nightmare come to life!"

"Oh sure, I know you. I've been married to your sister for 46 years."

Top Ten Reasons Why It's Great to Be from Nova Scotia

10. It's the only place in North America to get bombed in a war, though it was by a munitions ship that caught on fire.
9. Your province is shaped like male genitalia.
8. Everyone is a fiddle player.
7. If someone asks if you're a Newfie, you are allowed to kick their ass.
6. The local hero is an insane, fiddle-playing, sexual pervert.
5. The province produced Rita MacNeil, the world's largest land mammal.
4. You are the reason Anne Murray makes money.
3. You can pretend to have Scottish heritage as an excuse to wear a kilt.
2. The economy is based on fish, lobster and fiddle music.
1. Even though it smells like dead sea animals, Halifax is considered Canada's most beautiful city.

St. John's newscast: "This just in! There was a terrible tragedy down at the local curling club. They all drowned during spring training."

Overheard in a Newfoundland bar: "I'm on a screech diet. I've lost three days already."

Nova Scotia Lobster Man

After spending all day on the water, a fisherman is walking to his car from the pier carrying two lobsters in a bucket. A fisheries officer approaches him and asks to see his fishing licence.

The fisherman says to the officer, "I did not catch these lobsters. They are my pets. Everyday I come down to the water and whistle, and these lobsters jump out so I can take them for a walk, only to return them at the end of the day."

The officer, not believing him, reminds him that it is illegal to fish without a licence. The fisherman turns to the officer and says, "If you don't believe me, then watch," and he throws the lobsters back into the water.

The officer says, "Now whistle to your lobsters and show me that they will come out of the water."

The fisherman turns to the officer and says, "What lobsters?"

Q: Why did the lobster blush?

A: Because he saw the ocean's bottom.

A Newfie Abroad

A Newfie wants to marry a sheik's daughter in Egypt. The sheik says to the Newfie, "You have to complete three tasks before you can marry her."

The Newfie replies, "That sounds good."

So then the sheik says, "There are three tents. In the first tent, there is a 40-ounce bottle of rum, which you have to drink in a half-hour."

The Newfie replies, "Piece of cake."

"In the second tent," says the sheik, "is a sabre-toothed tiger that needs his tooth pulled."

The Newfie replies, "Easy."

"And in the third tent," the sheik says, "there is a women that has never been sexually pleasured before, and you have to pleasure her."

The Newfie replies, "Not a problem."

So the Newfie walks into the first tent, and a half-hour later, he walks out and says, "Well, that was easy enough. Show me the next tent."

He walks into the second tent, and the tent starts to shake. Strange noises start coming from within. A few minutes later, there is silence. The Newfie walks out of the tent, bleeding and with his clothes all ripped, and says, "Now, where's that woman who wants her tooth pulled?"

Q: *What did the Newfie fisherman say to the magician?*

A: *Pick a cod, any cod.*

Looking for Work

A company is looking to hire someone for an important position, so they interview dozens of applicants and narrow their search down to three people from different parts of the country.

In an attempt to choose one, they give all three applicants the same question, which they must answer within 24 hours. The one with the best response gets the job.

Q: Why are some fish at the bottom of the ocean?

A: Because they dropped out of their school.

The question: "A man and a woman are in bed, nude. The woman is lying on her side with her back facing the man, and the man is lying on his side facing the woman's back. What is the man's name?"

After the 24 hours are up, the three applicants are brought in to give their answer.

The first, from Vancouver, says, "My answer is, there *is* no answer."

The second, from Toronto, says, "My answer is that there is no way to determine the answer with the information we were given."

The third one, from Newfoundland, says, "I'm not exactly sure, but I have it narrowed down to two names. It's either Willie Turner or Willie Nailer."

The Newfoundlander gets the job.

Newfie on a Business Trip

A Newfie checks into a hotel on a business trip and is a bit lonely, so he decides to get one of those girls you see advertised in phone booths when you're calling for a cab. He grabs a card on his way in to the hotel. It is an ad for a girl calling herself Erogonique, a lovely girl bending over in the photo. She has all the right curves in all the right places, beautiful long wavy hair, long graceful legs all the way up—you know the kind. So he's in his room and figures, what the heck, he'll give her a call. "Hello?" the woman says. *Wow! She sounds sexy.*

"Hi, I hear you give a great massage, and I'd like you to come to my room and give me one. No, wait, I should be straight with you. I'm in town all alone and what I really want is sex. I want it hard, I want it hot and I want it now. I'm talking kinky the whole night long. You name it, we'll do it. Bring implements, toys, everything you've got in your bag of tricks. We'll go hot and heavy all night. Tie me up, wear a strap-on, cover me in chocolate syrup and whipped cream, anything you want, baby. Now, how does that sound?"

She says, "That sounds fantastic...but for an outside line, sir, you need to press 9."

> "An optimist in Canada is someone who think things could be worse."
>
> –Former Reform Leader Preston Manning

Captured

A Québecker, an Albertan and a Newfie are swimming in the sea when suddenly they are captured by pirates. The captain tells them, "You are going to be locked up in dungeons for 50 years, but I'm not heartless, so I'll give you something to go in with."

The Québecker says he wants booze, so he goes in with his booze.

The Albertan says he wants some women, so he goes in with his women.

Finally, the Newfie says he wants cigarettes, so he goes in with his cigarettes.

Fifty years later, the Québecker comes out of his dungeon pissed, the Albertan comes out with his women and kids and the Newfie comes out and says "Got a light?"'

A girl from Newfoundland and a girl from Toronto are seated side by side on an airplane. The girl from Newfoundland, being friendly and all, says: "So, where ya from, b'y?"

The Toronto girl says, "From a place where they know better than to use a preposition at the end of a sentence."

The girl from Newfoundland girl sits quietly for a few moments and then replies with a sweet smile and her fabulous sticky-sweet drawl, "So, where ya from, bitch?"

Speeder

The Pope is visiting New Brunswick in his limo and says to the driver, "Why don't you let me drive for once."

The driver thinks to himself, *Well, I can't say no to this guy. He's the pope.* So the driver pulls over, and they change places. The Pope is having fun, hauling butt down the highway, dodging cars. After a while, the driver taps on the window and tells the Pope, "Slow down a bit. You might get pulled over."

The Pope says, "Ahhh, don't worry about it. I'm the Pope." He rolls up the window and continues to drive fast. After a few moments, he gets pulled over. The cop walks to the car, and the Pope rolls down the tinted window.

The cop sees the Pope and says, "Oh, I, ehhh, sorry, can you hold on a minute?"

"Sure," the Pope says.

The cop walks back to his car and radios the station. He says, "Guys, I just pulled over someone really important."

Q: *What's the difference between a Newfie wedding and a Newfie funeral?*

A: *One less drunk.*

They ask, "Who? The Prime Minister?"

"No, more important."

"The president of another country?"

"No, even more important."

"Well, who is it?"

"I don't know, but the Pope is his chauffeur."

Plane Crash

Newfoundland's worst air disaster occurred early this morning when a small two-seater Cessna plane crashed into a cemetery. Newfie search-and-rescue workers have recovered 1826 bodies so far and expect that number to climb as digging continues into the night.

A defendant is on trial for murder in Charlottetown. There is strong evidence indicating his guilt, but no corpse has been found.

In the defence's closing statement, the lawyer, knowing that his client will probably be convicted, resorts to a trick.

"Ladies and gentlemen of the jury, I have a surprise for you," the lawyer says as he looks at his watch. "Within one minute, the person presumed dead in this case will walk into this courtroom."

He looks toward the courtroom door. The jurors, somewhat stunned, all look on eagerly. A minute passes. Nothing happens.

Finally the lawyer says, "Actually, I made up the previous statement. But you all looked on with anticipation. I, therefore, put it to you that there is reasonable doubt in this case as to whether anyone was killed and insist that you return a verdict of not guilty."

The jury, clearly confused, retire to deliberate. A few minutes later, the jury returns and pronounces a verdict of guilty.

"But how?" inquires the lawyer. "You must have had some doubt. I saw all of you stare at the door."

The jury foreman answers, "Oh, we looked. But your client didn't."

Legendary

It's the final examination for an introductory English course at Dalhousie. The exam is two hours long, and booklets are provided. The professor is very strict and tells the class that any exam not on his desk in exactly two hours will not be accepted, and the student will fail. A half-hour into the exam, a student comes rushing in and asks the professor for an exam booklet.

"You're not going to have time to finish this," the professor warns as he hands the student a booklet.

"Yes, I will," replies the student. He takes a seat and begins writing. When the two hours are up, the professor calls for the exams, and all the students line up to hand them in, except for the late student, who continues writing. A half hour later, the last student goes up to the professor, who is sitting at his desk preparing for his next class. The student tries to put his exam on the stack of booklets.

"No, you don't," says the professor. "I'm not accepting that. It's late." The student looks incredulous and angry.

"Do you know who I am?"

"No, as a matter of fact, I don't," replies the professor.

"DO YOU KNOW WHO I AM?" the student asks again.

"No, and I don't care," replies the professor with an air of superiority.

"Good," replies the student, and he quickly lifts the stack of completed exams, stuffs his in the middle and walks out of the room.

Did you hear about the Newfie that stayed up all night studying for a blood test?

Three Men on a Farm

Three men are travelling in rural New Brunswick when their car breaks down. They seek shelter at the nearest farmhouse.

The farmer has only two spare beds, so he informs the men that one of them will have to sleep in the barn.

One of the men, a very polite Hindu mathematician, immediately volunteers and goes out to the barn. A short time later, there is a knock on the door, and sure enough, there stands the mathematician, very apologetically explaining that there are cows in the barn, and because of his religious convictions, he doesn't think he can remain there.

The second man, a conservative rabbi, volunteers to take his place. Out he goes, but a short time later, there is a knock on the door. Sure enough, he, too, is back, explaining that because there is a pig in the barn, he will be quite uncomfortable out there.

Finally, the third man, a practicing lawyer, agreeably proceeds out to the barn. In a little while, there is a knock on the door. And when the farmer answers it, sure enough, there are the cows and the pig.

A condom company is thinking about relocating their manufacturing plant to Newfoundland. The board of directors is currently deciding whether to move the plant to Conception Bay, Dildo or Come-by-Chance.

Out Hunting

Two Newfies go duck hunting. Five hours pass with no luck. Finally, one of the men says to the other, "Maybe we ought to try throwing the dogs a little bit higher."

Q: *Why do men like Newfie jokes?*

A: *Because they can relate to them.*

Game of Wits

An English professor from Dalhousie and a Newfie are the two finalists in a poetry competition. For the final contest, they have to write a poem in two minutes containing a word that is given to them by the judges. The word is "TIMBUKTU."

> **Q:** *How do you confuse a Newfie?*
>
> **A:** *You don't—they are born that way.*

The Dalhousie professor is the first to recite his poem:

Slowly across the desert sand,
Trekked a lonely caravan.
Men on camels two by two,
Destination Timbuktu.

The audience goes wild. They figure the Newfie doesn't stand a chance against an English professor.

Nevertheless, the Newfie stands up and recites his poem:

Me and Tim a-hunting went,
Met three whores in a pop-up tent.
They were three and we were two,
So I bucked one and Tim-bucked-two.

The Newfie wins hands down.

A Newfie decides one day that she is sick and tired of Newfie jokes and how all Newfies are perceived as stupid, so she decides to show her husband that Newfies really are smart.

She decides that while her husband is off at work, she will paint a couple of rooms in the house.

The next day, right after her husband leaves for work, she gets down to the task at hand. Her husband arrives home at 5:30 PM and smells the distinctive odour of paint.

He walks into the living room and finds his wife lying on the floor in a pool of sweat. He notices that she is wearing a ski jacket and a fur coat at the same time. He goes over and asks her if she is okay. She assures him that she's fine.

> **Q:** *What do you get when you offer a Newfie a penny for his thoughts?*
>
> **A:** *Change.*

He asks what she is doing. She explains that she wants to prove to him that not all Newfies are dumb, and so she is painting the house. He then asks her why she is wearing both a ski jacket and a fur coat.

She replies, "The directions on the paint can say, 'For best results, put on two coats.'"

Good Son

An old man lives alone near Alberton, PEI. He wants to spade his potato garden, but it is very hard work. His only son, who used to help him, is in prison for selling drugs. The old man writes a letter to his son and describes his predicament.

Dear son,

I am feeling pretty bad because it looks like I won't be able to plant my potato garden this year. I'm just getting too old to be digging up a garden plot. If you were here, all my troubles would be over. I know you would dig the plot for me.

Love, Dad

A few days later, he receives a letter from his son.

Dear Dad,

For heaven's sake, Dad, don't dig up that garden, that's where I buried the bodies!

Your loving son

At 6:00 the next morning, the RCMP show up and dig up the entire area without finding any bodies. They apologize to the old man and leave.

That same day, the old man receives another letter from his son.

Dear Dad,

Go ahead and plant the potatoes now. That's the best I could do under the circumstances.

Your loving son

Just Another Day in PEI

One night, the Potato family—Mother Potato and her three daughters—sits down to dinner. Midway through the meal, the eldest daughter speaks up. "Mother Potato?" she says. "I have an announcement to make."

"And what might that be?" says Mother, seeing the obvious excitement in her eldest daughter's eyes.

"Well," replies the daughter, with a proud but sheepish grin, "I'm getting married!"

The other daughters squeal with surprise as Mother Potato exclaims, "Married! That's wonderful! And who are you marrying, Eldest Daughter?"

"I'm marrying a Russet!"

"A Russet!" replies Mother Potato with pride. "Oh, a Russet is a fine tater, a fine tater indeed!"

As the family shares in the eldest daughter's joy, the middle daughter speaks up. "Mother? I, too, have an announcement."

"And what might that be?" encourages Mother Potato.

Not knowing quite how to begin, the middle daughter pauses, then says with conviction, "I, too, am getting married!"

"You, too!" Mother Potato says with joy. "That's wonderful! Twice the good news in one evening! And who are you marrying, Middle Daughter?"

"I'm marrying an Idaho!" beams the middle daughter.

"An Idaho!" says Mother Potato with joy. "Oh, an Idaho is a fine tater, a fine tater indeed!"

Once again, the room comes alive with laughter and excited plans for the future. Suddenly, the youngest Potato daughter interrupts. "Mother? Mother Potato? Um, I, too, have an announcement to make."

"Yes?" says Mother Potato with great anticipation.

"Well," begins the youngest Potato daughter with the same sheepish grin as her eldest sister before her, "I hope this doesn't come as a shock to you, but I am getting married, as well!"

"Really?" says Mother Potato with sincere excitement. "All of my lovely daughters to be married! What wonderful news! And who, pray tell, are you marrying, Youngest Daughter?"

"I'm marrying Peter Jennings!"

"Peter Jennings?" Mother Potato scowls. "But he's just a common tater!

You Know You're from Prince Edward Island When...

- even though more people live on Vancouver Island, you still got the big-ass bridge.
- you can walk across the province in half an hour.
- you were probably once an extra on *Road to Avonlea*.
- you talk potatoes before you talk about the weather.
- the economy is based on fish, potatoes and CBC TV shows.
- tourists arrive, see the *Anne of Green Gables* house, then promptly leave.
- you play hockey in winter and golf in summer, spring and fall.
- it doesn't matter to you if Québec separates.
- you don't share a border with the Americans, or with anyone for that matter.
- even you forget this tiny island is a province.

At the Olympics

A Russian and a Newfie wrestler are set to square off for the Olympic gold medal. Before the final match, the Newfie wrestler's trainer comes to him and says, "Now, don't forget all the research we've done on this Russian. He's never lost a match because of this 'pretzel' hold he has. Whatever you do, do not let him get you in that hold or you're finished!"

The Newfie nods his acknowledgement. As the match starts, the Newfie and the Russian circle each other several times, looking for an opening.

All of a sudden, the Russian lunges forward, grabbing the Newfie and wrapping him up in the dreaded pretzel hold. A sigh of disappointment arises from the crowd, and the trainer buries his face in his hands, knowing all is lost. He can't watch the inevitable happen.

Suddenly, there is a scream, then a cheer from the crowd, and the trainer raises his eyes just in time to watch the Russian go flying up in the air. The wrestler's back hits the mat with a thud, and the Newfoundlander collapses on top of him, making the pin and winning the match.

The trainer is astounded. When he finally gets his wrestler alone, he asks, "How did you get out of that hold? No one has ever done it before!"

The wrestler answers, "Well, I was ready to give up when he got me in that hold, but at the last moment, I opened my eyes and saw this pair of testicles right in front of my face. I had nothing to lose, so with my last ounce of strength, I stretched out my neck and bit those babies just as hard as I could."

"So," the trainer exclaims, "that's what finished him off!"

"Not really. You'd be amazed how strong you get when you bite your own nuts."

A Polish man moves to Canada and marries a Halifax girl. Although his English is far from perfect, they get along very well. One day, he rushes into a lawyer's office and asks him to arrange a divorce for him. The lawyer says that getting a divorce will depend on the circumstances.

"Why do you want this divorce?" asks the lawyer.

"She going to kill me," says the Polish man.

"What makes you think that?"

"I got proof."

"What kind of proof?" wonders the lawyer.

"She going to poison me. She buy a bottle at drugstore and put on shelf in bathroom. I can read, and it say 'Polish Remover.'"

Happy Hour in Newfoundland

A Newfie sees a sign at a restaurant. It reads:

HAPPY HOUR SPECIAL: LOBSTER TAIL & BEER

"Lard thunderin' Jaises!" he says to himself. "Me three favourite things!"

Hockey Camp

A young Newfoundland-born player is drafted by the Habs and is ready to attend his first training camp.

"How will I get by?" he asks his father. "I don't speak French."

"Just speak slow," the old man says. "They understand you when you do that."

As the young man shows up at camp he walks up to another rookie and says, "Hi...my...name... is...John."

The other fella says, "Hi...my...name...is...Mark."

"Where...are...you...from?"

"New...found...land"

"Me...too"

"If...we're...both...from.. the...Rock...then... why...are...we...wasting... our...time...speaking... French?"

In Newfoundland on a golf tour, Tiger Woods drives his new Ford Fusion into a gas station in a remote part of the countryside. The pump attendant, who obviously knows nothing about golf, greets him in a typical Newfoundlander manner.

"Top of the mornin' to yer, sir," says the attendant.

Tiger nods a quick "hello" and bends forward to pick up

Q: *What bird gasps and pants around Newfoundland?*

A: *A Puffin.*

the nozzle. As he does so, two tees fall out of his shirt pocket onto the ground.

"What are dose?" asks the attendant.

"They're called tees," replies Tiger.

"Well, what on God's earth are dey for?" inquires the attendant.

"They're for resting my balls on when I'm driving," says Tiger.

"Lard thunderin'!" says the Newfoundlander. "Ford thinks of everyting!"

Robbery!

A Newfie and a Nova Scotian decide to rob a bank together. The Nova Scotian plans the robbery and goes over the plan extensively with the Newfie.

The robbery begins. The Nova Scotian drives up in front of the bank, stops the car and says to the Newfie, "I want to make absolutely sure you understand the plan. You are supposed to be in and out of the bank in no more than three minutes with the cash. Do you understand?"

"Perfectly," says the Newfie.

The Newfie goes in the bank while the Nova Scotian waits in the getaway car.

One minute passes...two minutes pass...then seven minutes pass, and the Nova Scotian guy is really stressing out.

Finally, the bank doors burst open, and out comes the Newfie. He has a safe wrapped up in rope and is dragging it to the car. About the time he gets the safe in the trunk car, the bank doors burst open again. The security guard comes out firing his weapon, with his pants and underwear down around his ankles.

As the guys are getting away, the Nova Scotian says, "Man, I thought you understood the plan!"

The Newfie says, "I did! I did exactly what you said!"

"No, you idiot," says the Nova Scotian man. "You got it all mixed up. I said tie up the GUARD and blow the SAFE!"

Getting Married

Jacob, age 92, and Rebecca, age 89, live in Fredricton and are excited about their decision to get married. They go for a stroll to discuss the wedding, and on the way, they pass a drugstore. Jacob suggests they go in.

Jacob addresses the man behind the counter. "Are you the owner?"

The pharmacist answers, "Yes."

Jacob: "We're about to get married. Do you sell heart medication?"

Pharmacist: "Of course we do."

Jacob: "How about medicine for circulation?"

Pharmacist: "All kinds."

Jacob: "Medicine for rheumatism and scoliosis?"

Pharmacist: "Definitely."

Jacob: "How about Viagra?"

Pharmacist: "Of course."

Jacob: "Medicine for memory problems, arthritis and jaundice?"

Pharmacist: "Yes, a large variety. The works."

Jacob: "What about vitamins, sleeping pills, Geritol and antidotes for Parkinson's disease?"

Pharmacist: "Absolutely."

Jacob: "You sell wheelchairs and walkers?"

Pharmacist: "All speeds and sizes."

Jacob: "We would like to use this store as our bridal registry."

Top 25 Things You'll Never Hear a Maritimer Say

25. "I'll take Shakespeare for 1000, Alex."
24. "Duct tape won't fix that."
23. "Come to think of it, I'll have a Heineken."
22. "We don't keep firearms in this house."
21. "You can't feed that to the dog."
20. "No kids in the back of the pickup. It's not safe."
19. "Wrasslin's fake."
18. "I'll have grapefruit instead of fried baloney."
17. "Who's Jimmy Flynn?"
16. "Give me the small bag of dulse."
15. "Moose heads detract from the decor."

14. "Spittin' is such a nasty habit."
13. "Trim the fat off that steak."
12. "The tires on that truck are too big."
11. "I'll have the arugula and radicchio salad."
10. "I've got it all on a USB stick."
9. "Would you like your fish poached or broiled?"
8. "My fiancée is registered at Tiffany's."
7. "Checkmate."
6. "Please, no more lobster."
5. "Does the salad bar have bean sprouts?"
4. "I don't have a favourite hockey team."
3. "My truck will never make through that mud bog."
2. "Rita who?"
1. "I couldn't find a thing at Canadian Tire today."

CHAPTER THREE

Québec: There's One in Every Family

Ontario versus Québec

Two men, one from Ontario and one from Québec, are in a cave when they come across a magic lamp.

As they fight over who the lamp belongs to, a genie pops out.

The genie says, "I shall grant each of you one wish and only one, so make it good."

> **Q:** *What's the difference between France and Québec?*
>
> **A:** *Québec has prettier women and colder beer.*

The Québecois speaks first. "I want you to build 100-foot wall around the border of Québec. This will ensure that the English culture does not corrode our superior heritage."

The genie nods, "Done." He then turns to the Ontarian. "And your wish?"

"Fill it with water."

Changing Identity

An Ontarian wants to become a Newfie, so he goes to a neurosurgeon and says, "Is there anything you can do to make me a Newfie?"

"Sure," says the surgeon. "All I have to do is cut out one-third of your brain."

The man agrees to the procedure, but during the operation the surgeon's knife slips and instead of cutting out one-third of the brain, he accidentally removes two-thirds. The surgeon is embarrassed by his error and waits by the patient's bedside for him to wake up. Finally, the man stirs in his bed and opens his eyes.

> **Q**: *Why do Québeckers do it doggie style?*
>
> **A**: *So they can both watch the Canadiens game.*

"I'm very sorry, but instead of cutting out one-third of your brain, I accidentally cut out two-thirds," says the surgeon.

To which the patient replies, "Qu'est-ce que vous avez dit, monsieur?"

Québecker on Vacation

A Québecois staying in a hotel in Edmonton phones room service for some pepper. "Black pepper or white pepper?" asks the hotel clerk.

"Toilette pepper!" yells the Québecois.

A young Canadian boy finds a French beret and tries it on for a few laughs. He goes to show his mom and says, "Look, Mom, I'm Québecois." Outraged, she slaps him hard on the cheek and shouts, "Go tell your granny what you just said."

The boy finds his grandma and shows her his beret. "Look Granny, I'm Québecois."

A look of rage passes over her face, and she slaps the boy hard on the cheek. "I can't believe you just said that!" she shouts. "Go and repeat it to your father."

> **Q:** *How does a separatist change a light bulb?*
>
> **A:** *He holds it in the air and the world revolves around him.*

Crying, the kid finds his father and says, "Look Dad, I'm Québecois." His dad says nothing but picks up a stick and spanks him on the bum. "What do you have to say for yourself now?" asks his dad when he is finished beating him.

The boy screams back, "I've only been Québecois for five minutes, and I already hate all you damn Anglos!"

Graffiti on a Montréal Wall

JESUS SAVES!

Richard gets the rebound,

He Shoots! He Scores!

Pauline Marois, long retired from public life, moves to Spain to get away from it all. Once settled, she gets into a conversation with her neighbour, who is as outspoken and opinionated as she is.

"So you come from Québec. I understand hockey is the most popular sport there. In Spain, we find it barbaric."

"Monsieur," says Marois. "I am surprised by your words. After all, in your country, the most popular sport is bullfighting. Québeckers find that sport more barbaric. Also, you expressed that hockey is the most popular sport in Québec. You are wrong on all accounts—*revolting* is!"

Retired Snowbirds

Francine and Pauline—two elderly Québec widows now residing in Florida—are curious about the latest arrival in their retirement apartment block. He is a quiet, handsome gentleman who likes to keep to himself.

> **Q:** *What's the difference between a bad cold and a separatist?*
>
> **A:** *You can get rid of a bad cold.*

One day, Francine says, "Pauline, you know I'm shy. Ever since I lost my Maurice, I cannot talk to men. Why don't you go talk to him and find out more about who he is? He looks lonely."

So Pauline goes over to talk to the man as he sits beside the apartment's pool. She says shyly, "My friend and I were wondering why you look so lonely."

"Of course I am lonely," he answers. "I've spent the past 20 years in prison."

Shocked, Pauline asks, "*Zut Alors!* Why?"

"I strangled my third wife."

"*Tabarnac!* What happened to your second wife?"

"I shot her."

"*Calice!* What happened to your first wife?"

"We had a fight and she fell off a building."

"*Saint Ciboire!*"

Pauline then walks back to Francine and says, "It's okay, Francine. He's single."

At the Bell Centre

A hockey fan has a lousy seat and cannot really get a good view of the game, but through his binoculars he can see an empty spot just behind the Canadiens bench. So he goes down and asks the man sitting next to the empty seat if it is taken.

"This is my wife's seat," he replies solemnly. "She passed away. She was a big Habs fan."

"I'm terribly sorry to hear of your loss. May I ask why you didn't give the ticket to a friend or a relative?"

"I couldn't. They're all at the funeral."

"In English-speaking Canada, hockey sometimes seems to be the sole assurance that we have a culture. That is something never in question in Québec."

–Rick Saluting, playwright, in the Preface to *Les Canadiens*

Neglected Wife

A wife is having an affair with the TV repairman. She complains, "My husband never pays any attention to me—all he cares about is watching those damned Montréal Canadiens play hockey on

TV. That's why we've got the biggest TV in the world—just so he can watch the games."

Just then, she hears a key in the front door. Her husband has come home early. She looks to her lover and says, "Quick, hide behind the television."

So the lover hides behind the TV, and the husband walks into the room and sits down to watch the hockey game. After 10 minutes, the repairman is so hot and uncomfortable that he steps out from behind the TV and walks straight past the husband and out the door.

The husband turns to his wife, who is sitting beside him with a look of fear in her eyes, and says, "Hey honey, did you see why the referee sent that guy off?"

Knock, knock!

Who's there?

Québec.

Québec who?

Québec to the end of the line.

Gouvernement du Québec Answering Machine (Translated)

Hello, you have reached the government of Québec.

For Québecois calling from inside Québec, press 1.

For Québecois calling from outside Québec, press 2.

If you are English, you are out of luck.

A federalist resident of rural Québec dies and goes to heaven. He is greeted at the gates by St. Peter.

"Well, *mon ami,* what did you do to glorify your country?" asks St. Peter.

The man replies, "I'll tell you what I did. On the day of the Festivale du St. Jean Baptiste, I walked down the street carrying a Canadian flag and a picture of the Queen, and I sang 'Oh Canada.'"

St. Peter looks at the man with surprise and asks him, "When was that?"

The man looks at his watch and says, "About two minutes ago."

Q: What two books of the Old Testament best describe Québec history?

A: Lamentations and Exodus.

Québec Corruption

At the height of a Québec political corruption trial, a prosecuting attorney attacks a witness. "Isn't it true," he bellows, "that you accepted $5000 to compromise this case?"

The witness stares out the window as though he hasn't heard the question.

"Isn't it true that you accepted $5000 to compromise this case?" the lawyer repeats loudly.

The witness still does not respond.

Finally, the judge leans over and says, "Sir, please answer the question."

"Oh," the startled witness says. "I thought he was talking to you."

Alouettes Fireman

Larry, a star player for the Montréal Alouettes, is jogging down the street when he sees a building on fire. A lady is standing on a third-storey ledge holding her pet cat in her arms.

"Hey lady!" yells Larry. "Throw me the cat!"

"No!" she cries. "It's too far!"

"I play football. I can catch him!"

The smoke is pouring from the windows, so finally the woman waves to Larry, kisses her cat goodbye and tosses it down to the street.

Larry keeps his eye on the cat as it comes plunging down toward him. The feline bounces off an awning, and Larry runs into the street to catch it. He jumps almost 2 metres into the air and makes a spectacular, one-handed catch. The crowd that has gathered to watch the fire breaks into cheers. Larry does a little dance, lifts the cat above his head, wiggles his knees back and forth, then spikes the cat into the pavement.

Maurice's favourite sport is driving around in his truck hitting Anglos. One day as Maurice is out running over Anglos and having tonnes of fun, he sees a priest hitchhiking on the side of the road.

Mistaking him for an Anglo, Maurice almost hits him but swerves away at the last second. Feeling terrible, Maurice offers to give the priest a ride.

While Maurice and the priest are driving along with neither of them saying much, Maurice sees an Anglo walking along. Getting all excited, Maurice speeds up in hot pursuit, but at the very last second, Maurice remembers the priest sitting in his truck and swerves out of the way. Relieved to have missed the Anglo, Maurice turns to the priest and says, "Father, I almost hit an Anglo!"

"Don't worry, *mon petit,*" the priest replies. "I got him with my door."

Two assassins are hired to kill the boss of the Montréal mafia. They follow his every move for months and find out that every day at noon he goes outside and does his stretching exercises.

So the assassins set up shop right across the street, get all of their sights set, load the guns and have everything ready to go.

Noon comes, no boss...10 minutes longer...still no boss.

One assassin turns to the other and says, "Gee, I hope nothing happened to him."

Hometown Drivers

A Torontonian returns home after living in Québec for one year. Back in Toronto driving around his familiar streets, he is proceeding through an intersection when a car runs a red light and crashes into him.

He escapes without injury, but his car is completely totalled. He walks over to the other driver and complains angrily, "For a full year, I lived in Québec, where they are supposed to have the worst drivers in all of Canada, and I didn't get a single scratch on my car. I'm back for one day in bloody Toronto, and you come along and almost kill me. What the hell is the matter with you, buddy?"

The guilty driver looks up with a furrowed brow and says, "Quoi? Je ne parle pas l'Anglais!"

Two Indians and a Québecker are walking along together in the forest, when, all of sudden, one of the Indians spots a cave in a hill in the distance. He runs up to it and hollers into the cave, "Woooo! Woooooo! Wooooo!" Then he listens very closely, until he hears an answer come back, "Wooooo! Wooooo! Wooooo!"

With that, he tears off his clothes and runs into the cave.

The Québecker is puzzled by this display and asks the other Indian, "What was that all about? Is he nuts?"

"No," replies the other Indian. "It is mating time for us. When we see a cave, we yell 'Wooooo! Woooo! Wooooo!' If we hear that answer back, it means there is a woman in the cave waiting for us to come make love to her."

The Indian spots another cave, runs over and bellows, "Woooo! Wooooo! Wooooooo!" Then off come the clothes and into the cave he goes.

The Québecker starts walking around searching for a cave of his own. When he finally sees one, he thinks, "Man! Look at the size of this cave! The most beautiful Indian woman must be hiding on the inside."

He takes off and at the mouth of the cave he begins to holler, "Wooooo! Woooo! Wooooo!" He listens and just a second later he hears the answering call, "WOOOOOO! WOOOOOO! WOOOOOOO!" In a second, the Québecker is naked and runs into the cave with a big smile on his face.

The next day, the local local paper's headline reads, "Naked Québecker Run Over by Freight Train."

> "I read and learned and fretted more about Canada after I left than I ever did while I was home. I absorbed anything I could on topics that ranged from folklore to history to political manifestos...I ranted and raved and seethed about things beyond my control. In short I acted like a Canadian."
>
> –Will Ferguson

Lovers on a Plane

A Vancouverite and a Calgarian are seated next to a Montréaler on an overseas flight. After a few cocktails, the men begin discussing their home lives.

"Last night, I made love to my wife four times," the Vancouverite brags, "and this morning she made me delicious crêpes and told me how much she adores me."

"Ah, last night," the Calgarian says, "I made love to my wife six times, and this morning she made me a wonderful omelette and told me she could never love another man."

When the Montréaler remains silent, the Vancouverite smugly asks, "And how many times did you make love to your wife last night?"

"Once," he replies.

"Only once?" the Calgarian arrogantly snorts while the Vancouverite laughs. "And what did she say to you this morning?"

"She said, 'I guess we had better stop—it's time to get up.'"

Reaching the end of a job interview, the Human Resources person asks a young engineer fresh out of McGill University, "What starting salary were you thinking about?"

The engineer says, "In the neighbourhood of $125,000 a year, depending on the benefits package."

The interviewer says, "Well, what would you say to a package of five weeks vacation, 14 paid holidays, full medical and dental, company-matching retirement fund to 50% of salary and a company car leased every two years—say, a red Corvette?"

The engineer sits up straight and says, "Wow! Are you kidding?"

The interviewer replies, "Yeah, but you started it."

Lesson Learned

First-year students at McGill University Medical School are receiving their first anatomy class with a real dead human body. They gather around the surgery table, where the body is covered with a white sheet. The professor starts the class by saying, "It is necessary to have two important qualities as a doctor. The first is that you should not be disgusted by anything involving the human body."

The professor pulls back the sheet, sticks his finger in the anus of the corpse, withdraws it and sticks it in his mouth.

"Go ahead and do the same thing," he tells his students. The students initially freak out and hesitate for several minutes but eventually take turns sticking a finger in the anus of the corpse and sucking on it.

When everyone has taken a turn, the professor looks at the class and tells them, "The second most important quality is observation. I stuck in my middle finger but sucked on my index finger. Now learn to pay attention!"

A Different Hunt

An old man in rural Québec is sitting on his front porch watching the sunrise. He sees the neighbour's kid walk by carrying something big under his arm. He yells out, "Hey boy, what you got there?"

The boy yells back, "A roll of chicken wire."

The old man asks, "What you gonna do with that?"

The boy says, "Gonna catch some chickens."

The old man yells, "You damn fool. You can't catch chickens with chicken wire!"

The boy just laughs and keeps walking.

That evening at sunset, the boy comes walking by and, to the old man's surprise, is dragging behind him the chicken wire with about 30 chickens caught in it.

Same time the next morning, the old man is out watching the sunrise and sees the boy walk by carrying something round.

The old man yells out, "Hey boy, what you got there?"

The boy yells back, "Roll of duct tape."

The old man asks, "What you gonna do with that?"

The boy says back, "Gonna catch me some ducks."

The old man yells back, "You damn fool. You can't catch ducks with duct tape!"

The boy just laughs and keeps walking.

That night around sunset, the boy comes walking by and, to the old man's amazement, is trailing behind him the unrolled roll of duct tape with about 35 ducks caught in it.

Same time the next morning, the old man sees the boy walking by carrying what looks like a long reed with something fuzzy on the end.

The old man says, "Hey boy, what you got there?"

The boy says, "It's a pussy willow."

The old man says "Wait up...I'll get my hat."

Montréal's Underside

A young man picks up a Montréal prostitute for his first taste of sex. The madam suggests that he start with 69. He decides to give it a try. The prostitute leads him to a room, gets undressed and instructs the young man on what to do. Unfortunately, just as he starts, she farts. The man quietly says to himself, "Phew," but he goes down on her again. A moment later, she farts again. He says, "Phew," but continues. Once more, she farts. This time, he immediately gets up and starts walking out.

She asks him what's wrong, and he replies, "I don't think I can take another 66 of those!"

A rural Québecker is on trial for killing his wife when he caught her with a neighbour. When asked why he shot her instead of her lover, he replies, "Ah, m'sieur, is it not better to shoot a woman once than a different man every week?"

Quick Thinking

A man in a Florida supermarket tries to buy half a head of lettuce. The young produce assistant tells him that they sell only whole heads of lettuce. The man persists and asks to see the manager. The boy says he'll ask his manager about it.

Walking into the back room, the boy says to his manager, "Some asshole wants to buy half a head of lettuce."

As he finishes his sentence, he turns to find the man standing right behind him, so he adds, "And this gentleman has kindly offered to buy the other half."

The manager approves the deal, and the man goes on his way. Later the manager says to the boy, "I was impressed with the way you got yourself out of that situation earlier. Here, we like people who think on their feet. Where are you from, son?"

"Québec, sir," the boy replies.

"Well, why did you leave Québec?" the manager asks.

The boy says, "Sir, there's nothing but whores and hockey players up there."

"Really?" says the manager. "My wife is from Québec."

"No sh*t?" replies the boy. "Who'd she play for?"

This is How We Do It

At a local college dance, a guy from Québec asks a girl from Sweden to dance. While they are dancing, he gives her a little squeeze and says, "In Québec, we call this a hug."

She replies, "Yaah, in Sveden, we call it a hug too."

A little later, he gives her a peck on the cheek and says, "In Québec, we call this a kiss."

She replies, "Yaah, in Sveden, we call it a kiss too."

Toward the end of the night, and a lot of drinks later, he takes her out on the campus lawn, has sex with her and says, "In Québec, we call this a grass sandwich."

She says, "Yaaah in Sveden, we call it a grass sandwich, too, but we usually put more meat in it."

Caught a Big One

A kind-hearted fellow is walking through downtown Montréal and is astonished to see an old man, fishing rod in hand, fishing in a fountain.

"Tch, Tch!" says the passer-by to himself. "What a sad sight. That poor old man is fishing over a bed of flowers. I'll see if I can help."

So the kind fellow walks up to the old man and asks, "What are you doing, my friend?"

"Fishin', sir."

"Fishin', eh? Well, how would you like to come have a drink with me?"

The old man stands, puts his rod away and follows the kind stranger to the corner bar. He orders a large glass of beer and a fine cigar.

His host, the kind fellow, feels good about helping the old man, and he says, "Tell me, old friend, how many did you catch this morning?"

The old fellow takes a long drag on the cigar, blows a careful smoke ring and replies, "You are the sixth today, sir."

Pierre and François, two avid fishermen and well-known drunks, are out in a boat on their favourite lake, not catching anything and polishing off a few beers. Suddenly, Pierre gets what he thinks is a nibble, but upon reeling it in, he finds only an old oil lamp. When he rubs off some of the dirt to get a better look at the lamp, a genie appears out of thin air.

The genie says, "I'll grant you a single wish."

Pierre thinks for a second and says, "I wish this whole lake was Labatt Blue." And *poof* his wish comes true! The lake is now filled with his favourite beer.

François looks at his friend in disgust, "*Tabarnac!* Now we have to piss in the boat!"

A French missionary is trying to convert the chief of the Iroquois to his particular form of Catholicism. He asks the chief, "When you die, don't you want to go to heaven?"

"No," replies the chief. "If heaven was any good, you French would have already grabbed it."

Another Visitor at the Pearly Gates

St. Peter is working at his desk when he is surprised to see a Québecker approaching him. He is not expecting an arrival until a little later in the day.

"How did you get up here," he asks.

The Québecker replies, "Flu."

In a small Québec town, a rather sizeable factory hires only married men. Concerned about this policy, a local woman calls on the manager and asks him, "Why is it that you limit your employees to married men? Is it because you think women are weak, dumb, cantankerous or what?"

"Not at all, ma'am," the manager replies. "It is because our employees are used to obeying orders, are accustomed to being shoved around, know how to keep their mouths shut and don't pout when I yell at them."

Red-light District

In a Montréal nursing home, one of the old women is running up and down the hall, flipping her nightgown up and down and yelling "Supersex! Supersex!"

She sees an old man sitting in a wheelchair outside his room, runs up to him and pulls up her nightie. "Supersex! Supersex!"

He looks at her for a moment contemplating and then says, "I think I'll have the soup."

A plane is on its way to Montréal when a blonde in economy class gets up, moves to the first-class section and sits down. The flight attendant sees her and asks to see her ticket. She then tells the blonde that because she paid for economy, she will have to sit in the back. The blonde replies, "I'm blonde, I'm beautiful, I'm going to Montréal and I'm staying right here."

The flight attendant goes into the cockpit and tells the pilot and co-pilot that some blonde bimbo sitting in first class belongs in economy and won't move back to her seat. The co-pilot goes back to the woman and tries to reason with her.

The blonde replies, "I'm blonde, I'm beautiful, I'm going to Montréal and I'm staying right here." The co-pilot returns to the cockpit and tells the pilot that he should probably have the police waiting to arrest the woman when they land.

The pilot says, "I'll handle this. I'm married to a blonde. I have learned to speak 'blonde.'" He goes back to the woman, whispers in her ear and, without question, she gets up and moves back to her seat in the economy section. The flight attendant and co-pilot are amazed and ask him what he said to make her move without any fuss. "I told her first class isn't going to Montréal."

Vive la Difference!

Three contractors are bidding to fix a broken fence at city hall in Montréal. One is from Montréal, another from Québec City and the third from Gatineau. They go with a city official to examine the fence.

The Gatineau contractor takes out a tape measure and does some measuring, then works some figures with a pencil. "Well," he says. "I figure the job will cost about $900: $400 for materials, $400 for my crew and $100 profit for me."

The Québec City contractor also does some measuring and figuring, then says, "I can do this job for $700: $300 for materials, $300 for my crew and $100 profit for me."

The Montréal contractor doesn't measure or figure but leans over to the city official and whispers, "I'll do it for $2700."

The official, incredulous, says, "You didn't even take any measurements! How did you come up with such a high figure?"

The Montréal contractor whispers back, "Well, $1000 for me, $1000 for you and we hire the guy from Québec City to fix the fence."

Hazardous Foods

A doctor addresses a large audience in Québec City. "The stuff we put into our stomachs is so toxic it should have killed most of us years ago. Red meat is awful. Soft drinks corrode your stomach lining. Chinese food is loaded with MSG. High fat diets can be disastrous, and none of us realizes the long-term harm caused by the germs in our drinking water. But one food is the most dangerous of all, and we all have, or will, eat it. Can anyone tell me which food causes the most grief and suffering for years after you've eaten it?"

After several seconds of quiet, a 75-year-old man in the front row raises his hand and softly says, "Wedding cake."

Georges Patrie of Longueuil, Québec, is going to bed when his wife tells him that he left the light on in the shed. Georges opens the door to go turn off the light but sees people in the shed in the process of stealing things. He immediately phones the police.

They ask, "Is someone in your house?"

Georges says no and explains the situation. The police tell him that all patrols are busy, so he should simply lock his door and an officer will be there when one is available.

Georges says, "Okay," and hangs up. He counts to 30 and phones the police again.

"Hello, I just called you a few seconds ago because there were people in my shed. Well, you don't have to worry about them now because I've just shot them all."

Then he hangs up. Within five minutes, three squad cars, an armed response unit and an ambulance show up. Of course, the police catch the burglars red-handed.

One of the policemen says to Georges, "I thought you said that you'd shot them!"

Georges says, "I thought you said there was nobody available."

A Strange Meeting

During a recent outing in Montréal, a woman sneaks off to visit a fortune-teller of some local repute. In a dark and hazy room, peering into a crystal ball, the mystic delivers grave news. "There's no easy way to say this, so I'll just be blunt. Prepare yourself to be a widow. Your husband will die a violent and horrible death this year."

Visibly shaken, the woman stares at the fortune-teller's lined face, then at the single flickering candle, then down at her hands. She takes a few deep breaths to compose herself. She simply has to know. She meets the fortune-teller's gaze, steadies her voice and asks, "Will I be acquitted?"

A female Montréal police officer arrests a guy for drunk driving. While reading him his rights, the officer tells the man, "Sir, you have the right to remain silent. Anything you say, can and will be held against you."

"Boobs," the drunk replies.

Ever wonder how many Québecois it takes to change a light bulb?

Well, that is a difficult question. First, a commission will have to be formed to study the issue at a cost of $5 million; then the bids will have to go to the contractors, who will artificially inflate the cost of changing the light bulb and deliver kickbacks to the politicians; then the Office de la Langue Français will have to investigate whether everyone on the job is speaking French. Then maybe one foreman will screw in the light bulb while 10 union guys take their breaks. Once installed, the bulb will fall out because of improper installation, and another commission will look into the causes. Ten years after the original request, the light bulb will finally be installed, but it won't always work, and when an Anglophone enters the room, it'll shut off.

Captured

An American, an Englishman and a Québecker are captured by cannibals. The chief comes to them and says, "The bad news is that we're going to kill you. We will put you in a pot, cook you, eat you and then use your skins to build a canoe. The good news is that you can choose how to die."

The American says, "I'll take the sword." The chief gives him a sword. The American says, "God bless the USA!" and stabs himself to death.

The Englishman says, "A pistol for me, please." The chief gives him a pistol. Pointing it at his head, the Englishman says, "God save the queen!" and blows his brains out.

The Québecker says, "Gimme a fork." The chief is puzzled, but he shrugs and gives him a fork. The Québecker takes the fork and starts jabbing himself all over—his stomach, sides and chest. Blood gushes all over.

The chief is appalled and asks, "What are you doing?"

The Québecker responds, "So much for your canoe, you stupid jerk!"

A Québecker falls off a ladder and breaks his leg so badly that he cannot go to work. In fact, it is so bad that he will have to use a wheelchair for the rest of his life.

The WCB is suspicious of his claim and sends an inspector to visit him. The inspector warns, "We will pay the claim, but we will follow you around 24 hours a day, and if we establish that your claim is bogus, we will have you arrested and thrown in jail."

The Québecker replies, "Then are you going to be following me to the St. Phillipe Church of Holy Miracles, and there you will see the greatest miracle in your life."

SOVEREIGNTY!!!!!!!!!!!!

Québec finally holds its third referendum on separation, and when the votes are counted, it is clear that the majority of Québec has voted for the province to secede from Canada.

Stephen Harper and Pauline Marois agree to negotiate the separation of Québec and the breaking up of the federation. The negotiations are held behind closed doors, but they do not go smoothly. The meetings are tense and fraught with emotion. The nation watches and waits to see what will become of the country.

After a few days, Harper emerges from a meeting and tells the television cameras, "Don't worry everyone. We are almost finished. There is only one more thing for us to agree on. Canada has agreed to let Québec go its own way, but Québec has not yet agreed to take the Maritimes with them."

Chapter Four

Ontario and Manitoba: Stuck in the Middle

You Know You're From Ontario if...

- you think Toronto is the capital of Canada.
- you haven't celebrated a Stanley Cup win in more than 40 years.
- you decide who will win the federal election.
- you measure distance in hours.
- you think $500,000 for a condo in Toronto is a good deal.
- you learn French from when the Leafs or the Sens play the Canadiens.
- you can say, "I didn't realize how bad the smog was getting until they started making highway signs in Braille."

Electric Car

A Torontonian buys an electric car, but he's unhappy with its performance, so he calls up the dealer to complain. "My car will only go 10 metres!" he says to the salesman.

The salesman runs through some checks with him. "Is the battery charged up? Are the brakes off? Is it in gear?"

The Torontonian confirms that everything seems to be working fine. The salesmen cannot figure out the problem.

"Why do you say it only goes 10 metres?" asks the salesman.

"Because that's as far as the cord will stretch to the plug," says the Torontonian.

In Hell

Two guys from Toronto die and wake up in hell. The next day, the devil stops in to check on them and sees them dressed in parkas, mittens and toques, warming themselves around the fire. The devil asks, "What are you doing? Isn't it hot enough for you?"

The two guys reply, "Well, you know, we're from Canada, the land of snow, ice and cold. We're just happy for a chance to warm up a little bit, eh?" The devil decides that the men aren't miserable enough and turns up the heat.

The next morning, he stops in again and there they are, still dressed in parkas, toques and mittens. The devil says to them, "It's awfully hot down here. Can't you guys feel it?"

Again the two guys reply, "Well, like we told ya yesterday, we're from Canada, the land of snow, ice and cold. We're just happy for a chance to warm up a little, eh?" This gets the devil a bit steamed up, and he decides to fix these two guys. He cranks the heat up as high as it will go.

People are wailing and screaming everywhere. He stops by the room with the two guys from Canada and finds them in light jackets and bucket hats, grilling bacon and drinking beer. The devil is astonished. "Everyone down here is in abject misery, and you two seem to be enjoying yourselves," he says.

The two Canadians reply, "Well, ya know, we don't get too much warm weather up there in Canada, so we've just *got* to have a cook-out when the weather's *this* nice." The devil is absolutely furious. He can hardly see straight.

Q: *If a loonie and a toonie are on top of the CN Tower, which one jumps off first?*

A: *The loonie, because it has less cents.*

Finally, he comes up with the answer. The two guys love the heat because they have been cold all their lives, so the devil decides to turn off all the heat in hell. The next morning, the temperature is below zero. Icicles are hanging everywhere, and people are shivering so badly that they are unable to do anything but wail, moan and gnash their teeth. The devil smiles and heads for the room with the two Canadians. He finds them back in their parkas, toques and mittens.

But now they are jumping up and down, cheering, yelling and screaming like mad men. The devil is dumbfounded. "I don't understand," he says. "When I turn up the heat, you're happy. Now it's freezing cold, and you're still happy. What's up with you two?"

The guys from Toronto look at the devil in surprise. "Don't you know, eh? If hell freezes over, it must mean the Maple Leafs have won the Stanley Cup!"

A Maple Leaf Fan Takes a Test

A Toronto Maple Leaf fan reports to his university final exam, which consists of "yes/no" type questions. He takes his seat in the exam room and stares at the paper for five minutes. In a fit of inspiration, he takes out his wallet, removes a loonie and tosses it, marking the answer sheet: "yes" for heads and "no" for tails. Within 30 minutes, he's done, whereas the rest of his classmates are still hunched over their papers, sweating it out. During the last few minutes of the exam, the moderator notices the Maple Leaf fan desperately throwing the coin and muttering to himself.

"What are you doing? Are you okay?" asks the moderator.

"I finished the exam in a half an hour," he replies, "but I'm rechecking my answers and none of them match!"

Two guys from Ottawa, Robert and Maurice, decide that life in Ottawa has gotten too dull, so they plan a trip to Manitoba to shoot moose. They fly in commercial planes all the way to Winnipeg, and from there, they hire a bush pilot to take them into moose country.

The pilot puts them down on a short airstrip about 200 kilometres from nowhere.

Q: *What is the best lake in Canada?*

A: *Lake Superior*

"Boys," he says, "I'll be back here at noon in three days. You be right here, and remember that this plane is too small to carry more than the three of us and *one* moose. So, there's no need to hunt more than one moose, because you'll be able to take only one out of here."

Robert and Maurice nod their agreement and off the plane goes, leaving the two guys in the wilderness, eager for their hunting expedition.

Three days later, the plane lands at 11:55 local time, and there beside the airstrip are Robert and Maurice, each sitting on a moose, grinning broadly.

"Okay," says the pilot, "which moose are we going to take back?"

"Why, both of them," says Robert. "We got to take both back to show that we are both as good as each other."

"No, no, NO," says the pilot. "I told you that the plane could bring back only *one* moose."

"What's the matter?" asks Maurice. "Ain't your plane good enough to carry one little ol' extra moose? We got two on a plane just like this one last year."

"Fine," says the pilot. "Ain't nobody going to out-fly me around here. If you got two moose on that plane, you can get two moose on my plane."

So, they load up and take off. But the plane, as predicted, can't handle the extra load, and they crash.

"There are too many nasty little self-centred nations in the world already; God forbid that Canada should add to the number!"

–W.L. Grant

The two guys from Ottawa wake up in adjacent treetops, and Robert asks, "Where are we?"

Maurice responds, "About 100 metres farther that we were last year!"

Cheek Replacement

A vain, well-off married Toronto couple are in a terrible car accident on the 401. The husband is lucky enough to escape with only a few minor injuries, but the wife's face is severely burned. The doctors tell the husband that they can't graft any skin from her body because she is too skinny. So the husband offers to donate some of his own skin. However, the only skin deemed suitable by the doctors is on his buttocks. The husband and wife agree to keep that detail to themselves and go ahead with the procedure.

After the surgery, everyone is astounded by the woman's transformation. She's even more beautiful than before. Her friends and relatives cannot stop complementing her on her new-found beauty.

One day when she is alone with her husband, she becomes overwhelmed by his sacrifice.

"Dear, I just wanted to thank you for everything," she says. "You sacrificed your body for my beauty, and I love you for it. There is no way I can repay you."

"My darling," says the husband. "Think nothing of it. I get all the thanks I need every time I see your mother kiss you on the cheek."

The Jumper

A Métis man from Manitoba is driving across a bridge in his pickup truck when he notices a man standing on the edge, ready to jump to his death.

The Métis man stops his truck, runs up to the man and says, "Hey, why are you doing this?"

The man replies, "I have nothing to live for."

"Well, think of your wife and children!"

"I have no wife and no kids," replies the jumper.

"Then think of your mother and father," says the Métis man.

"Mom and Dad are dead!"

The Métis man thinks harder, looks over at the man and says, "Well, then, think of the noble Louis Riel!"

The jumper asks, "Who's that?"

"Who? WHO?!?" demands the Métis man. "You might as well jump, you damn pale face!"

Q: How did the Torontonian break his leg playing for the Toronto Maple Leafs?

A: He fell out of the tree.

A missionary who has spent years showing a Manitoba Cree Native tribe how to farm and build things to be more self-sufficient gets the word that he is to return home.

He realizes that the one thing he never taught the tribe was how to speak English, so he goes for a walk in the forest with the chief. He points to a tree and says, "This is a tree."

The chief looks at the tree and grunts, "Tree." The missionary is pleased with the response.

They walk a little farther, and the padre points to a rock and says, "This is a rock."

Hearing this, the chief looks and grunts, "Rock." The padre is getting really enthusiastic about the results when he hears a rustling in the bushes. He peeks over the top and sees a couple in the midst of heavy sexual activity.

The padre is really flustered and quickly says, "Riding a bike."

The chief looks at the couple briefly, pulls out his blowgun and kills them both.

The padre goes ballistic and yells at the chief, saying that he has just spent years teaching the tribe how to be civilized and kind to each other, so how could the chief kill these people in cold blood that way?

The chief replies, "Riding *my* bike."

Hot Day

Jack lives in Windsor, Ontario, with his wife. As he gets out of the shower on a particularly hot day, he says to his wife, "It's just too hot to wear clothes today, honey. What do you suppose the neighbours would think if I mowed the lawn like this?"

"Probably that I married you for your money."

A senior citizens' group charters a bus from Windsor to Gananoque. As they enter the town, an elderly woman comes up to the driver and says, "I've just been molested!"

The driver believes she must have fallen asleep and had a dream. He tells her to go back to her seat and sit down.

A short time later, another old woman comes forward and claims that she was just molested. The driver figures he must have a busload of old wackos. Who would molest those old ladies?

About 10 minutes later, a third old lady comes up and says she's been molested, too. The bus driver decides that he's had enough and pulls into a rest area.

When he turns on the interior lights and stands up, he sees an old man on his hands and knees crawling through the aisles.

"Hey gramps, what are you doing down there?" says the bus driver.

"I lost my toupee. I thought I found it three times, but every time I grab it, it runs away."

Queen's Visit

Queen Elizabeth II is visiting one of Toronto's finest hospitals, and during her tour of the wards, she passes a room where one of the male patients is masturbating.

"Oh God," says the Queen. "That's disgraceful. What is the meaning of this?"

The doctor leading the tour explains, "I am sorry your Royal Highness, but this man has a very serious condition in which his testicles fill up rapidly with semen. If he doesn't do what he is doing at least five times per day, he could swell up and might die"

"Oh, I am sorry," says the Queen. "I was unaware that such a medical condition existed."

On the same floor, they pass another room where a young, blonde nurse is performing oral sex on another patient.

"Oh, my God," says the Queen. "What's happening here?"

The doctor replies, "Same problem, better insurance plan."

A burglar breaks into a house in Winnipeg. He sees a Blu-ray player that he wants, so he takes it. Then he hears a voice saying, "Jesus is watching you."

He looks around with his flashlight, muttering, "What the hell was that?" Then he sees some cash on a table and takes it. Once again, he hears a voice say, "Jesus is watching you."

He hides in a corner, trying to locate the source of the voice and spots a birdcage with a parrot in it. He goes over and asks, "Was that your voice?"

The bird says, "Yes."

"What's your name?" the burglar asks.

The parrot says, "Moses."

The burglar says, "What kind of person names his bird Moses?"

The parrot replies, "The same person who names his Rottweiler Jesus."

Separation of Church and State

The Ten Commandments display is to be removed from the Supreme Court building in Ottawa. There is a good reason for the move. You can't post "Thou Shalt Not Steal, Thou Shalt Not Commit Adultery and Thou Shall Not Lie" in a building full of lawyers and politicians without creating a hostile work environment.

The madam opens the brothel door to see a rather dignified, well-dressed, good-looking man in his late 40s or early 50s. "May I help you?" she asks.

"I want to see Valerie," the man replies.

"Sir, Valerie is one of our most expensive ladies. Perhaps you would prefer someone else," says the madam.

"No, I must see Valerie," is the man's reply.

Just then, Valerie appears and announces to the man that she charges $1000 per visit. Without hesitation, the man pulls out the money, gives it to Valerie and goes upstairs with her. After an hour, the man calmly leaves.

The next night, the same man appears again, demanding to see Valerie. Valerie explains that no one ever comes back two nights in a row—it's too expensive and there are no discounts. The price is still $1000. Again the man pulls out the money, gives it to Valerie and goes upstairs with her. After an hour, he leaves.

> **Q:** *What is 74 to a Canadian prostitute?*
>
> **A:** *69 plus tax.*

The following night, the man is there again. Everyone is astounded that he has come for the third consecutive night, but he pays Valerie and they go upstairs. After their session, Valerie questions the man. "No one has ever been with me three nights in a row. Where are you from?" she asks.

The man replies, "Winnipeg."

"Really?" she says. "I have family in Winnipeg."

"I know," the man says. "Your father died, and I am your sister's attorney. She asked me to give you your $10,000 inheritance."

Student Life

Two university students, Frank and Matt, are riding on a Toronto subway when a beggar approaches them asking for spare change.

Frank adamantly rejects the man in disgust.

Matt, on the other hand, whips out his wallet, pulls out a couple of singles and hands them over to the beggar with a smile.

The beggar thanks him kindly and then continues on to the other passengers.

Frank is outraged by his friend's act of generosity.

"What on earth did you do that for?" shouts Frank. "You know he's only going to use it on drugs or booze."

Matt replies, "And we weren't?"

Albert Einstein arrives at a party and introduces himself to the first person he sees, asking, "What is your IQ?"

The man answers, "It is 241."

"That is wonderful!" says Albert. "We will talk about the Grand Unification Theory and the mysteries of the universe. We will have much to discuss!"

Next, Albert introduces himself to a woman and asks, "What is your IQ?"

The lady answers, "It is 144."

"That is great!" says Albert. "We can discuss politics and current affairs. We will have much to discuss!"

Albert then goes to another person and asks, "What is your IQ?"

The man answers, "Um, 51."

Albert ponders this for a moment and then says, "Go Maple Leafs!"

First Timers

Two Scottish nuns who have spent their lives cloistered arrive in Toronto by boat, and one says to the other, "I hear that the people of this country actually eat dogs."

"Odd," her companion replies, "but if we shall live in Toronto, we might as well do as the Torontonians do."

Nodding emphatically, the mother superior points to a hot dog vendor, and they both walk toward him. "Two dogs, please," says one.

The vendor is only too pleased to oblige, wraps both hot dogs in foil and hands them over the counter. Excitedly, the nuns hurry to a bench and begin to unwrap their "dogs."

The mother superior is first to open hers. She begins to blush and then, after staring at it for a moment, leans to the other nun and whispers cautiously, "What part did you get?"

Swimming Challenge

A brunette, a redhead and a blonde enter a race to cross Lake Ontario doing only the breaststroke. After approximately 14 hours, the brunette crawls up on the shore and is declared the fastest breaststroker. About 40 minutes later, the redhead emerges from the water gasping for breath and is declared the second-place winner. Nearly five hours later, the blonde finally comes ashore and collapses in front of worried onlookers.

When the reporters ask her why it took so long to complete the race, she replies, "I don't want to sound like a sore loser, but I think those other two girls were using their arms."

Passing Train

A man has to attend a large convention in Toronto. On this particular trip, he decides to bring his wife. When they arrive at their hotel and are shown to their room, the man says: "You rest here while I register. I'll be back within an hour."

The wife lies down on the bed, but just then, a train passes by close to the window and shakes the room so hard she's thrown off the bed. Thinking it must have been a freak occurrence, she lies down once more. Again a train shakes the room so violently that she's pitched to the floor.

Exasperated, she calls the front desk and asks for the manager. The manager says he'll be right up. He is skeptical, but the wife insists the story is true.

"Look, lie here on the bed. You'll be thrown right to the floor!" So the manager lies down next to the wife.

Just then, the husband walks in. "What are you doing here?" he says.

The manager replies, "Would you believe I'm waiting for a train?"

A couple from Ottawa decided to go to Miami Beach for a few days to thaw out during a particularly cold winter. The airline has strict frequent flyer rules, and the wife ends up on a flight the day after her husband.

The husband makes it down to Florida and arrives at his hotel. Upon getting to his room, he opens his laptop and sends his wife an email. Unfortunately, he doesn't notice that he has misspelled his wife's email address

In Red Deer, Alberta, a widow has just returned from the funeral of her husband, an Evangelical pastor of many years who had been called to glory just a few days earlier.

She decides to check her email because she is expecting to hear from relatives and friends. Upon reading the first email, she lets out a loud scream and faints. The woman's son rushes into the room and finds his mother on the floor. He glances up at the computer screen and sees the following email message:

To My Loving Wife,

I've just been checked in. Everything has been prepared for your arrival here tomorrow. Looking forward to seeing you then.

Your Devoted Husband

P.S. Sure is hot down here.

A Trip to McDonald's

A German tourist walks into a McDonald's in Toronto and orders a beer. In Germany and many parts of Europe, McDonald's actually does serve beer, so to him, this is perfectly normal. The local guy in line behind him immediately gives him a jab: "They don't serve beer here, you moron!"

The German fellow feels pretty stupid but suddenly turns to the Torontonian with a surprised look and begins to chuckle.

"And what's so funny?" the local demands.

"Oh, nothing really. I just realized that you came here for the food."

A family is on a train together.

Mother: "Why, John, this is the same train we took on our honeymoon to Niagara Falls."

Little Boy: "Dad, was I with you on that trip?"

Father: "Yes, son. You went up with me and came back with your mother."

Sports Fishing

On a tour of Florida, the Pope takes a couple of days off to visit the coast for some sightseeing. He is cruising along the beach in the Popemobile when there is a commotion just off shore. A man wearing a Toronto Maple Leafs jersey is frantically struggling to free himself from the jaws of a huge shark.

As the Pope watches, horrified, a speedboat comes racing up with three men aboard, all wearing Ottawa Senators jerseys. One quickly fires a harpoon into the shark's side. The other two reach out and pull the bleeding, semiconscious Leafs fan from the water. Then using baseball bats, the three heroes beat the shark to death and haul it into the boat.

Immediately the Pope shouts and summons them to the beach. "I give you my blessing for your brave actions," he tells them. "I heard that there is some bitter hatred between Senators and Leafs fans, but now I have seen with my own eyes that this is not the truth."

As the Pope drives off, the harpooner asks his buddies, "Who was that?"

"It was the Pope," one replies. "He is in direct contact with God and has access to all of God's wisdom."

"Well," the harpooner says, "he may have access to God's wisdom, but he doesn't know much about shark fishing. How's the bait holding up?"

A farmer in the Ontario countryside notices that a gentleman fishes at the lake close to the farmer's house and always leaves with a bucket full of fish. Strangely, the fellow has a boat, but a fishing pole is nowhere to be seen.

The farmer mentions the situation to the lake ranger. The ranger starts watching the man and realizes that everything the farmer told him was true. The man arrives at the lake in the morning without a fishing pole, and by early afternoon, he has a bucket full of fish.

One day, the ranger dresses like a fisherman and approaches the man. They exchange pleasantries, and the stranger asks the ranger to come fish with him. They travel for 45 minutes and arrive at a secluded spot. The stranger then pulls out a stick of dynamite.

One Manitoba farmer says to the other, "Wow, your crops are fit as a fiddle this year!"

The other says, "Thanks. That's music to my ears."

The ranger says, "I'm going to have to place you under arrest. I am a ranger, and you are fishing illegally!"

The stranger calmly lights the stick of dynamite, hands it to the ranger and says, "Are you gonna talk or fish?"

Flying Blind

One day at Pearson Airport, the passengers on an Air Canada airliner are seated, waiting for the cockpit crew to show up so the flight can get under way.

The pilot and co-pilot finally appear in the rear of the plane and begin walking up to the cockpit through the centre aisle. Both appear to be blind.

The pilot is using a white cane, bumping into passengers right and left as he stumbles down the aisle, and the co-pilot is using a guide dog. Both men wear huge sunglasses. At first, the passengers do not react, thinking that it must be some sort of practical joke. However, after a few minutes, the engines start spooling up, and the airplane moves down the runway.

The passengers whisper uneasily among themselves and look to the flight attendant for reassurance. Then the airplane starts accelerating rapidly, and people begin panicking.

Some passengers are praying, and as the plane gets closer to the end of the runway, the voices become more and more hysterical. Finally, when the airplane has less than 6 metres of runway left, there is a sudden change in the pitch of the shouts as everyone screams at once, and at the very last moment, the airplane lifts off and is airborne.

Up in the cockpit, the co-pilot breathes a sigh of relief and turns to the captain, "You know, one of these days the passengers aren't going to scream, and we're gonna get killed!"

Texan Visitor

A Texan, while visiting Toronto, finds himself in the backseat of a taxi on the way to his hotel. Passing by the Royal York, the Texan asks the cab driver, "What's that building there?"

"That's the Royal York Hotel," replies the cabbie.

"The Royal York? How long did it take to build that?" asks the Texan.

"About 12 years," replies the cabbie.

"Twelve years? We build 'em twice as high, twice as wide and four times as long down in Texas, and we do it in six months."

A while later, the cab driver makes his way past the Metro-Toronto Convention Centre. "What's that building over there?" asks the Texan.

"That's the Metro Toronto Convention Centre," replies the cabbie.

"Convention Centre? How long did it take to build that?" asks the Texan.

"About three years," replies the cabbie.

"Three years? We build 'em twice as high, three times as long and four times as wide down in Texas, and it only takes us about two weeks."

Shortly thereafter, the cabbie drives past the CN Tower. "What's that building there?" asks the Texan, pointing at the tower.

"Danged if I know," replies the cabbie. "It wasn't here when I drove by yesterday."

Tipper

A Winnipeg man stops by a café for breakfast. After paying the tab, he checks his pockets and leaves his tip—three pennies. As he strides toward the door, his waitress muses, only half to herself, "You know, you can tell a lot about a man by the tip he leaves."

The man turns around, curiosity getting the better of him. "Oh, really? Tell me, what does my tip say about me?"

"Well, this penny tells me you're a thrifty man."

Barely able to conceal his pride, the man utters, "Hmm, true enough."

> **Q:** *How do you know when you're staying in a Manitoba hotel?*
>
> **A:** *When you call the front desk and say, "I've gotta leak in my sink," the person at the front desk says, "Go ahead."*

"And this penny, it tells me you're a bachelor."

Surprised at her perception, he says, "Well, that's true, too."

"And the third penny tells me that your father was one, too."

Two men are drinking in a bar at the top of the CN Tower. One turns to the other and says, "You know, last week I discovered that if you jump from the top of this building, by the time you fall half way, the winds are so intense that they carry you around the building and back in through the window at the halfway point." The bartender just shakes his head in disapproval as he wipes the bar.

The second man says, "Are you nuts? There is no way in heck that could happen."

The first man says, "No, it's true. Let me prove it to you." So he gets up from the bar, jumps off the balcony and careens toward the street below.

When he passes the halfway point, the wind whips him around the building and back in through the window, and he takes the elevator back up to the bar.

The second man says, "You know, I saw that with my own eyes, but it must have been a fluke."

> Did you hear about the $3,000,000 Manitoba Provincial Lottery? The winner gets $3 a year for a million years.

The first man replies, "No, I'll prove it again." And again he jumps and hurtles toward the street until the halfway point, where the wind gently carries him around the building and in through the window. Once upstairs, he urges his fellow drinker to try it.

The second man says, "Well, what the heck. It works. I'll try it." So he jumps off the balcony, plunges downward, passes the halfway point and hits the sidewalk with a splat.

Back upstairs, the bartender turns to the first man. "You know, Superman, you're a real jerk when you're drunk."

Last Wishes

A man is struck by a bus on a busy street in Toronto. He lies dying on the sidewalk as a crowd of spectators gather around.

"A priest. Somebody get me a Catholic priest!" the man gasps. A policeman checks the crowd, but there is no priest, no minister or no man of God of any kind.

"A priest, please!" the dying man says again.

Then out of the crowd steps a little old Jewish man about 80 years old.

> You know you're in Manitoba when you slap a mosquito and it slaps you back.

"Mr. Policeman," says the man. "I'm not a priest. I'm not even a Catholic. But for 50 years now, I've lived behind St. Elizabeth's Catholic Church on Spadina, and every night I listen to the Catholic litany. Maybe I can be of some comfort to this man."

The policeman agrees and guides the octogenarian over to the dying man. The old man kneels down, leans over the injured man and says in a solemn voice, "B-4...I-19...N-38...G-54...O-72."

⋞ CHAPTER FIVE ⋟

Them Prairie Folk

Prairie Visitor

An American couple from Montana decide to go to Canada for their holidays one summer. They drive north across the border, stop at a dinosaur park then continue northeast. After driving for a couple of days, they realize they are lost. They find a small city and pull over to ask a pedestrian for directions.

"Hey buddy, can you tell us where we are?"

The pedestrian smiles, says "Saskatoon, Saskatchewan," and goes on his way.

The driver turned to his wife and says, "Well, we still don't know where we are. He doesn't even speak English."

After years of planning, an Albertan has finally saved up enough money for a trip to Paris. His first destination is the Eiffel Tower. Looking at the structure curiously, he turns to the tour guide and says, "How many barrels a day do you get out of her?"

> An Alberta RCMP pulls over a pickup truck on Highway 2. He asks the driver "Got any ID?"
>
> The driver says, "'Bout what?"

Two Saskatoon Buddies

First guy: "Hey did you hear about Randy?"

Second guy: "Nah, what's up with him?"

First guy: "Well, Randy always wanted to see the world. So he joined the Navy and asked to be put in a submarine."

A rural police officer in Central Alberta drives to a farm where a farmer has called in to report the loss of 2025 pigs. After visiting the farm, the officer returns to the station to enter the details on the computer, but he forgets the details of the case and decides to call the farmer back.

> **Q:** *What do you call a Prairie boy with a sheep under each arm?*
>
> **A:** *A pimp.*

"Is it true, Mr. Williams, that you lost 2025 pigs?" asks the officer.

"Yeth," says the farmer with a lisp.

Satisfied, the officer hangs up the phone and types, "Subject lost two sows and 25 pigs."

A Little Travel

A woman from Prince Albert, Saskatchewan, is travelling in Southeast Asia and stops in a restaurant to sample the local cuisine. Looking at the menu, she is horrified by its most expensive item: bird's nest soup.

"Do you mean to say that this is actually a bird's nest?" she asks the waiter.

The waiter assures her that it is a nest the bird builds with its own saliva.

"Are you saying that I am supposed to eat saliva from a bird's mouth," she asks rhetorically. "I can't imagine anyone eating something that comes out of a bird's mouth."

Looking over the menu, the woman makes a new choice. "Oh, then just make me an egg sandwich."

Have you heard about the Saskatchewan farmer who packed up his things and went to live in the city when he learned the country was at war?

University of Saskatchewan Tests

The university football coach is addressing the newest rookie on the team in the dressing room and says, "Look, I know I'm not supposed to let you play because you failed math class, but we really need you on the team. So let's make a deal. If you can answer one simple math question, you can play. Okay?"

The rookie nods.

"Right," says the coach. "What's two plus two?"

The rookie thinks for a moment and answers, "Four."

But before the coach can say anything, the rest of the team starts protesting, "Oh, come on, coach, give him another chance."

Sleepy Husband

After spending all day watching football on TV, a Roughriders fan falls asleep in his chair and spends the night there. His wife wakes him up in the morning.

"It's twenty to seven," she calls out.

"Who's in the lead?"

Three married couples from Regina all die on the same day and arrive in heaven. St. Peter is waiting at the gates to take down their names. After telling St. Peter about all of her good work, the first husband tells him that his wife's name is Penny.

"I'm sorry," says St. Peter, "but I can't admit anyone with a name connected to money."

The next couple approaches St. Peter, and he commends the man for his charitable works. However, when the man says his wife's name is Brandy, St. Peter says, "I'm sorry, but I cannot admit anyone with a name linked to alcohol."

Hearing this, the last wife turns to her husband and says, "Dick, I don't think you're getting in."

Q: *How can you tell if an Alberta redneck is married?*

A: *There is dried chewing tobacco on both sides of his pickup truck.*

Too Much Time on the Ranch

Two Alberta newlyweds walk up to a hotel clerk and ask for a suite.

"Bridal?" asks the clerk.

The new bride blushes and says, "No thanks. I'll hold on to his shoulders until we get the hang of it."

Two newlyweds from Edmonton travel to a remote cabin near Jasper for their honeymoon. After booking in on Saturday, they are not seen again for five days. The elderly couple that runs the resort become concerned, so the husband decides to investigate. He goes and knocks on the cabin door, and a bleary-eyed young man answers.

"Are you two okay?" asks the old man. "No one has seen you since Saturday."

"Yes, we are fine," replies the young man. "We're living on the fruits of love."

"I thought so," replies the old man. "But would you mind not throwing the peelings out the window? They're choking the wildlife."

Old West Alberta

A cowboy rides into town and goes to the saloon for a few drinks. When he comes out again, his horse is gone. He storms back into the saloon and shouts, "Who stole my horse?"

There is no reply.

Getting angry, he yells again. "Right, if no one owns up to stealing my horse, I'm gonna do what I did in Saskatoon."

Still silence from the saloon.

The cowboy is fuming mad. "This is your last chance. If no one owns up to stealing my horse, I'm going to do what I did in Saskatoon."

Fearing the worst, the prankster runs out and retrieves the horse. "It's outside, mister. Don't be doing nothing foolish now," says one patron.

Back at the bar, the bartender's curiosity gets the better of him and he asks, "What did you do in Saskatoon?"

The cowboy responds in a whisper, "I walked home."

A man boards a plane in Calgary and takes his seat. When he looks up from his in-flight manual, he spies the most beautiful woman he has ever seen. When she sits down next to him, he becomes flustered and nervous. Eager to start a conversation, he blurts out, "So where are you headed today?"

She turns, smiles the prettiest smile ever and says, "I am going to the annual Nymphomaniacs Convention in Edmonton."

He can hardly believe his ears. Sitting in front of him is the most beautiful woman he has ever seen—fire red hair, green eyes, perfect body—and she is a nymphomaniac. Struggling to maintain his cool, he asks, "And what is your job at this convention?"

She looks deep into his eyes and replies, "I will be speaking about some popular myths about sex and sexuality."

"Really?" he says. "And what myths are those?"

She explains, "Well, one of the most popular myths is that black men have the biggest penises when in fact it is the Native American who holds that title. Another myth is that Frenchmen or Italians are the best lovers, but it is actually men of Irish ancestry who romance women the best."

"Interesting," he says.

"I'm sorry," she says, gently touching his arm. "I am talking all about sex, and I don't even know your name."

The man puts out his hand and says, "Tonto. Tonto O'Reilly."

Prairie Intelligence Test

A psychology doctoral student is performing some word association tests on a sex-obsessed patient for her final thesis.

"Okay, sir. I am going to say a word, and you respond with the first thing that comes to mind. Okay? Here we go. What do you think of when I say hockey?"

"Sex."

"When I say pencil?"

"Sex."

"When I say flag?"

"Sex."

"Vagina?"

"Saskatchewan!"

On an Alberta Road

A man is driving up a steep, narrow mountain road. A woman is driving down the same road. As they pass each other, the woman leans out the window and yells, "PIG!!"

The man immediately leans out his window and replies, "BITCH!!"

They each continue on their way, and as the man rounds the next bend, he crashes into a pig in the middle of the road.

A minister is seated next to a cowboy on a flight to Red Deer. After the plane is airborne, drink orders are taken. The cowboy asks for a whiskey and soda, which is brought and placed before him. The flight attendant then asks the minister if he would like a drink.

He replies in disgust, "I'd rather be savagely raped by a dozen brazen whores than let liquor touch my lips."

The cowboy hands his drink back to the attendant and says, "Me too. I didn't know we had a choice."

Two Alberta Rednecks in a Bar

Two guys meet up in a bar. The first one asks, "Did your hear the news? Mike is dead!"

"Woah! What the hell happened to him?"

"Well, he was on his way over to my house the other day, and when he arrived outside the house, he didn't brake properly. And boom—he hits the curb. The car flips over, and he crashes through the sunroof, goes flying through the air and smashes through my upstairs bedroom window."

"What a horrible way to die!"

"No, no, he survived that. That didn't kill him at all. So, he lands in my upstairs bedroom, and he's on the floor all covered in broken glass. Then he spots the big old antique wardrobe we have in the room and reaches up for the handle to try to pull himself up. He's just dragging himself up when bang, this massive wardrobe comes crashing down on top of him, crushing him and breaking most of his bones."

"What a way to go, that's terrible!"

"No, no, that didn't kill him. So he manages to get the wardrobe off him and crawls out onto the landing. He tries to pull himself up on the banister, but under his weight, the banister breaks and he goes falling down to the first floor. In mid-air, all the broken banister poles spin and fall on him, pinning him to the floor, sticking right through him."

"Now that is the most unfortunate way to go!"

"No, no, that didn't kill him, he even survived that. So he's on the downstairs landing, just beside the kitchen. He crawls into the kitchen, tries to pull himself up on the stove, but reaches a big pot of boiling hot water, and whoosh, the whole thing comes down on him and burns most of his skin off."

"Man, what a way to go!"

"No, no, he survived that, he survived that! So, he's lying on the ground, covered in boiling water, and he spots the phone and tries to pull himself up to call for help, but instead he grabs the light switch and pulls the whole thing off the wall. The water and electricity don't mix, so he gets electrocuted, 10,000 volts shot through him."

"Now that is one awful way to go!"

"No, no, he survived that..."

"Hold on now, just how the hell did he die?"

"I shot him!"

"You shot him? What the hell did you shoot him for?"

"He was wrecking my house."

An Alberta redneck gets a job at a toy factory on the assembly line making Tickle Me Elmo dolls. On his first day, everything seems to be going okay until there is a major hold-up in the line at his workstation.

The plant foreman goes over to see what the problem is. He sees that the redneck has a stack of little bags and a container full of marbles. He watches for a moment as the redneck puts two marbles in a little bag and then stitches them between Elmo's legs.

The foreman yells, "What are you doing?"

"Well, sir," says the redneck. "I was told to give each doll two test-tickles."

Tough Cowboy

Three Alberta cowboys are sitting around a campfire out on the lonesome prairie, each with the bravado for which cowboys are famous. A night of tall tales begins.

The first says, "I must be the meanest, toughest cowboy there is. Why, just the other day, a bull got loose in the corral and gored six men before I wrestled it to the ground, by the horns, with my bare hands."

The second can't stand to be bested. "That's nothing. I was walking down the trail yesterday and a rattler slid out from under a rock and made a move for me. I grabbed that snake with my bare hands, bit its head off and sucked the poison down in one gulp. And I'm still here today."

The third cowboy remained silent, slowly stirring the coals with his penis.

Caught in a Storm

Three dead bodies turn up at the mortuary, all with very big smiles on their faces. The coroner calls the police to tell them what has happened.

"First body: Québecker, 60, died of heart failure while making love to his mistress. Hence the enormous smile, Inspector," says the coroner.

"Second body: Newfie, 25, won $1000 in the lottery, spent it all on whiskey. Died of alcohol poisoning, hence the smile."

The inspector asks, "What of the third body?"

"Ah," says the coroner, "this is the most unusual one. Billy-Bob, a redneck from Alberta, 30, was struck by lightning."

"Why is he smiling, then?" inquires the inspector.

"He thought he was having his picture taken."

A guy with a black eye boards a plane bound for Regina and sits down in his seat. He notices immediately that the guy next to him has a black eye, too.

He says to the man, "Hey, this is a coincidence, we both have black eyes. Mind if I ask how you got yours?"

The other guy says, "Well, it just happened. It was a tongue-twister accident. See, I was at the ticket counter and this gorgeous blonde with great breasts was there. So instead of saying, 'I'd like two tickets to Regina,' I accidentally said, 'I'd like two pickets to Vagina.' So she socked me a good one."

The first guy replies, "Wow! This is unbelievable. Mine was a tongue-twister, too. I was at the breakfast table and I wanted to say to my wife, 'Please pour me a bowl of Corn Flakes, honey.' But I accidentally said, 'You have ruined my life, you evil, self-centred, fat-assed harpy.'"

A Saskatchewan farmer has an old rooster and thinks it might be time to get a younger rooster to service his hens. He gets the new bird and lets him loose with the old rooster. The young rooster goes right over to the old rooster and challenges him to a fight.

The old rooster says, "Sonny, I'm too old to fight. Just follow me around, and I'll show you the place." The young rooster agrees and starts to follow the old rooster around. The old rooster shows him the barn, then the hen house...then starts to run. The young rooster thinks the old rooster is trying to pull a quick one, so he chases madly after him.

All of a sudden, there is a loud *bang!* and there stands the farmer, muttering "Dang, that's the third gay rooster I've had to kill this month."

Be Careful

An Edmonton tourist goes on a trip to China. While in China, he is very sexually promiscuous and does not take any precautions. A week after arriving back home, he awakens one morning to find his penis covered with bright green and purple spots. Horrified, he immediately goes to see his doctor.

The doctor, never having seen anything like this before, orders some tests and tells the man to return in two days for the results. The man returns a couple of days later, and the doctor says, "I've got bad news for you. You've contracted Mongolian VD. It's very rare and almost unheard of here. We know very little about it."

The man looks a little relieved and says, "Well, give me a shot or something and fix me up, doc."

The doctor answers, "I'm sorry, there's no known cure other than to amputate your penis."

The man screams in horror, "Oh no! I want a second opinion!"

The doctor replies, "Well, it's your choice. Go ahead if you want, but surgery is your only choice."

The next day, the man seeks out a Chinese doctor, figuring he'll know more about the disease. The Chinese doctor examines his penis and proclaims, "Ah yes, Mongolian VD. Very rare disease."

The guy says to the doctor, "Yeah, yeah, I already know that, but what can you do? My Canadian doctor wants to operate and amputate my penis!"

The Chinese doctor shakes his head and laughs, "Stupid Canadian doctor! Western doctors always want to operate. Make more money that way."

"Then there's no need to operate? Oh, thank God!" the man replies.

"Yes!" says the Chinese doctor, "You no worry! Wait two weeks, it fall off by itself!"

A huge University of Alberta freshman decides to try out for the football team.

"Can you tackle?" asks the coach.

"Watch this," says the freshman and then runs smack into a telephone pole, shattering it to smithereens.

"Wow," says the coach. "I'm impressed. Can you run?"

"Of course, I can run," says the freshman. He's off like a shot, and in just over nine seconds, he has run a 100-metre dash.

"Great!" enthuses the coach. "But can you pass a football?"

The freshman hesitates for a few seconds and then replies, "Well, sir, if I can manage to swallow it, I don't imagine I'll have any choice but to pass it."

At the Stampede

A Newfie cowboy rides into Calgary for the Stampede on his brand-new horse and ties it to a post. He then lifts the horse's tail and kisses its back end. An old man sees what the Newfie is doing and asks why he just kissed the horse's rear end.

"It helps my chapped lips," replies the Newfie.

"You mean kissing a horse's ass cures 'em?" says the old man.

"It doesn't cure them," replies the Newfie cowboy. "But it stops me from licking them."

A Calgary lawyer is representing the railroad in a lawsuit filed by an old Alberta rancher. The rancher's prize bull is missing from the part of his ranch through which the railroad passes. The rancher claims that the bull must have been hit by the train, and he wants to be paid the fair value of the bull. The case is scheduled to be tried before the Justice of the Peace in the back room of the general store.

As soon as the rancher shows up, the attorney for the railroad pulls him aside and tries to get him to settle out of court. The lawyer does his best selling job, and finally the rancher agrees to take half of what he was asking.

After the rancher signs the release and takes the cheque, the young lawyer can't resist gloating a little over his success, telling the rancher, "You know, I hate to tell you this, old man, but I put one over on you in there. I couldn't have won the case. The engineer was asleep and the fireman was in the caboose when the train went through your property that morning. I didn't have one witness to put on the stand. I bluffed you!"

The old rancher replies, "Well, I'll tell you, young feller, I was a little worried about winning that case myself because that darned bull came home this morning."

Country Bar

A gay man walks into a Calgary country bar and says, "I just want everyone to know that I'm gay, but I won't hit on anyone. I just like country music."

The bartender says that it's okay, and the man stays.

The next day, the gay man comes back with another guy and says, "This is my brother. I just want everyone to know that we're gay, but we won't hit on anyone. We just like country music."

The bartender again says that is okay, and the men stay.

Again the next day, the man comes back, but this time he is with even more men and says, "These are my cousins and my brother. I just want everyone to know that we're gay, but we won't hit on anyone. We just like country music."

The bartender finally gets curious and asks, "Hey, doesn't *anyone* in your family like girls?"

The gay man replies, "Yeah, but she doesn't like country music."

Awful, Just Awful

An Alberta redneck farmer goes to the vet and says, "My horse is constipated."

The vet says, "Take one of these pills, put it in a long tube, stick the other end in the horse's ass and blow the pill up there."

The redneck farmer comes back the next day, and he looks very sick.

"What happened?" the vet says.

The farmer says, "The horse blew first."

A big-city lawyer goes duck hunting in rural Saskatchewan. He shoots a bird, but it falls into a farmer's field on the other side of a fence. As the lawyer climbs over the fence, an elderly farmer drives up on his tractor and asks him what he is doing.

The litigator responds, "I shot a duck and it fell in this field, and now I'm going to retrieve it."

The old farmer replies, "This is my property, and you are not coming over here."

The indignant lawyer says, "I am one of the best trial attorneys in Canada, and if you don't let me get that duck, I'll sue you and take everything you own."

The old farmer smiles and says, "Apparently, you don't know how we settle disputes in Saskatchewan. We settle small disagreements like this with the Three Kick Rule."

The lawyer asks, "What is the Three Kick Rule?"

The farmer replies, "Well, because the dispute occurs on my land, first I kick you three times and then you kick me three times and so on back and forth until someone gives up."

The attorney quickly thinks about the proposed contest and decides that he could easily take the old codger. He agrees to abide by the local custom.

The old farmer slowly climbs down from the tractor and walks up to the attorney. His first kick plants the toe of his heavy steel-toed work boot into the lawyer's groin and drops him to his knees. His second kick is to the midriff and sends the lawyer's last meal gushing from his mouth. The lawyer is on all fours when the farmer's third kick to his rear end sends him face-first into a fresh cow pie.

The lawyer summons every bit of his will and manages to get to his feet. Wiping his face with the arm of his jacket, he says, "Okay, now it's my turn.

The old farmer smiles and says, "Naw, I give up. You can have the duck."

Canmore Fishing Trip

A couple of guys from Canmore are in their fishing boat, pulling in a lot of fish.

One of them says, "This is a pretty good spot. We should mark it so we can find it again tomorrow." He takes out a marker and starts to mark the top of the water.

His friend says, "Don't be so stupid, eh. You can't mark the water. Mark the side of the boat."

Killing Time

Two Saskatchewan farmers, Joe and Bob, live as neighbours but don't like each other much. During a period of –30°C weather, Bob and Joe have nothing better to do, so they make a bet. Whoever can sit out on a window ledge with a bare ass for the longest time wins a bottle of vodka.

After two hours, Bob's wife comes home and asks Bob, "What are you doing?"

Bob explains and she says, "Come on...you will only freeze your ass off."

Bob refuses to quit because he wants to win the bet.

Then his wife gets an idea. "Let's change places when Joe is looking the other way."

Bob's wife puts on the same pullover and cap and trades places with Bob.

Half an hour later, Joe's wife comes home and asks him, "What are you doing?"

Joe tells her and says, "I am determined to win the bottle!"

"You are crazy. Come on in."

"Certainly not, I am already on the winning side. Bob lost his balls half an hour ago!"

A man's business trip is cancelled and he is at home with his rather nervous wife. They go to bed, and around midnight, the phone rings.

The man rolls over and answers. "Hello?... What?...How the hell should I know?!? I live in Regina."

He hangs up and his wife asks, "Who was it dear?"

"Just some idiot who wanted to know if the coast was clear."

Saving Lives

Two Alberta rednecks walk into a restaurant. While having a bite to eat, they talk about their moonshine operation.

Suddenly, a woman at a nearby table, who is eating a sandwich, begins to cough. And after a minute or so, it becomes apparent that she is in real distress. One of the hillbillies looks at her and says, "Can ya swallow?"

The woman shakes her head no.

Then he asks, "Can ya breathe?"

The woman begins to turn blue and shakes her head no.

The redneck walks over to the woman, lifts up her dress, yanks down her drawers and quickly gives her a lick with his tongue where the sun don't shine. The woman is so shocked that she has a violent spasm, and the obstruction flies out of her mouth. As she begins to breathe again, the redneck walks slowly back to his table.

His partner says, "Ya know, I'd heard of that there 'Hind Lick Maneuver' but I ain't never seen nobody do it!"

Fire!

An Albertan comes home and finds his house on fire. He rushes next door, telephones the fire department and shouts, "Hurry over here! My house is on fire!"

"Okay," replies the fireman, "How do we get there?"

"Shucks, don't you still have them big red trucks?"

A fellow from Regina wakes up in the hospital bandaged from head to foot.

The doctor comes in and says, "Ah, I see you've regained consciousness. Now you probably won't remember, but you were in a pile-up on the highway. You're going to be okay, you'll walk again and everything, but...something happened. I'm trying to break this gently, but the fact is your penis was chopped off in the wreck, and we were unable to find it."

> Did you hear that they have raised the minimum drinking age in Saskatchewan to 32?
>
> They want to keep alcohol out of the high schools.

The man groans, but the doctor goes on, "You've got $9000 in insurance compensation coming from Saskatchewan Government Insurance, and we have the technology now to build you a new penis that will work as well as your old one did—better in fact! But the thing is, it doesn't come cheap. It's $1000 per inch."

The guy perks up at this. "So," the doctor says, "It's for you to decide how many inches you want. It's something you should discuss with your wife, though. I mean, if you had a 5-incher before, and you decide to go for a 9-incher, she might be a bit put out. If you had a 9-incher before and you decide only to invest in a 5-incher this time, she might be disappointed. So it's important that she plays a role in helping you reach a decision."

The man agrees to talk with his wife.

The doctor comes back the next day. "So," says the doctor, "Have you spoken with your wife?"

"I have," says the man.

"And what is the decision?" asks the doctor.

"We're getting granite countertops."

Sensitivity Training

Three Albertans—Cooter, Pete and KC—are working up on a cell phone tower in Alberta. As they start their descent, Cooter slips, falls off the tower and dies instantly. As the ambulance takes the body away, Pete says, "Well, damn, someone should go and tell his wife."

KC says, "Okay, I'm pretty good at that sensitive stuff. I'll do it." Two hours later, he comes back carrying a case of Budweiser.

Pete says, "Where did you get that beer, KC?"

"Cooter's wife gave it to me," KC replies.

"That's unbelievable! You told the lady her husband was dead and she gave you beer?"

"Well, not exactly," KC says. "When she answered the door, I said to her, 'You must be Cooter's widow.' She said, 'You must be mistaken. I'm not a widow.' Then I said 'I'll bet you a case of Budweiser you are.'"

The Labour Relations Board suspects a farm owner in Saskatchewan is not paying proper wages to his staff and send an agent to interview him.

"I need a list of your employees and how much you pay them," demands the agent.

"Well, there's my hired hand who's been with me for three years. I pay him $600 a week plus free room and board. The cook has been here for 18 months, and I pay her $500 a month plus free room and board. Then there's the half-wit who works about 18 hours a day. I pay him $10 a week and buy him chewing tobacco," says the farmer.

"That's the guy I want to talk to, the half-wit," says the agent.

The farmer says, "That would be me."

Learned

Some aspiring psychiatrists are attending their first class on emotional extremes. "Just to establish some parameters, what is the opposite of joy?" says the professor to the student from Alberta.

"Sadness," says the student.

"And the opposite of depression?" he asks of the young lady from Ontario.

"Elation," she answers.

"And you, sir," he says to the young man from Saskatchewan. "How about the opposite of woe?"

The young man replies, "Sir, I believe that would be giddy-up."

An Alberta redneck buys a ticket and wins the lottery. He goes to Calgary to claim it, where the man verifies his ticket number.

"I want my $20 million," the redneck says.

The man replies, "No, sir. It doesn't work that way. We give you a million today, and then you'll get the rest spread out for the next 19 years."

The redneck says, "Oh, no. I want all my money right now! I won it, and I want it."

If you get a divorce in Saskatchewan, are you still brother and sister?

Again the man patiently explains that the redneck would get only a million dollars that day and the rest over the next 19 years.

The redneck, furious with the man, screams, "Look, I want my money! If you're not going to give me my $20 million right now, then I want my dollar back!"

Brokeback Bar

A cowboy walks into a bar during Stampede, and two steps in, he realizes it's a gay bar. He figures, "What the heck, I really need a drink."

When the gay waiter approaches, he says to the cowboy, "What's the name of your penis?"

The cowboy says, "Look, I'm not into any of that. All I want is a drink."

The gay waiter says, "I'm sorry, but I can't serve you until you tell me the name of your penis. Mine, for instance, is called Nike, for the slogan 'just do it'. That guy down at the end of the bar calls his Snickers, because it really satisfies."

The cowboy looks dumbfounded, so the bartender tells him he'll give him a second to think it over.

The cowboy turns to the man sitting to his left drinking a beer and asks, "Hey bud, what's the name of yours?"

The man looks back and says with a smile, "Timex."

"Why Timex?" the thirsty cowboy asks.

The fellow proudly replies, "'Cause it takes a lickin' and keeps on tickin'!"

A little shaken, the cowboy turns to the two men on his right, who happen to be sharing a fruity margarita, and asks, "So, what do you guys call yours?"

The first man turns to him and proudly exclaims, "Ford, because 'quality is job one.'" Then he adds, "Have *you* driven a Ford lately?"

The guy next to him says, "I call mine Chevy…'like a rock!'" And gives a wink.

Even more shaken by all this chatter, the cowboy has to think for a moment before he comes up with a name for his manhood. Finally, he turns to the bartender and exclaims, "The name of my penis is Secret. Now give me a damn beer."

The bartender brings a beer, and as he begins to pour it, he turns to the cowboy with a puzzled look and asks, "Why Secret?"

The cowboy says, "Because it's 'strong enough for a man but made for a woman!'"

Chapter Six

The Land of the Rocky Mountains

You Might be From BC if...

- you don't own a heavy winter coat.
- you think double-glazed windows are for those in Ontario with cold weather.
- you go broke just paying rent.
- that two bedroom fixer-upper house costs $750,000.
- it's November, it's raining, but you're still wearing Birkenstocks.
- you think the Canucks have a chance of winning the Cup.
- all your friends' names end in Lee and Patel.
- you smoke the best weed.
- David Suzuki is your god.
- you know how to pronounce Squamish, Osoyoos and Nanaimo.
- you know the difference between chinook, coho and sockeye salmon.
- you have actually used your mountain bike on a mountain.
- you know that Dawson Creek is a town, not a TV show.
- you can tell the difference between Japanese, Chinese, Vietnamese, Korean and Thai food.
- you know more people who own boats than air conditioners.

- you know all the important seasons: Winter, Still Raining (Spring), Road Construction (Summer) and Raining Again (Fall).
- the provincial flowers are mildew and weed.
- your co-worker has eight body piercings and none are visible.
- you make over $300,000 a year and still can't afford a house.
- you take a bus and are shocked when two people carry on a conversation in English.
- your child's third-grade teacher has purple hair and a nose ring and is named Breeze.
- you can't remember...is pot illegal?
- you've been to a baby shower that has two mothers and a sperm donor.
- you have a very strong opinion about where your coffee beans are grown and can taste the difference between Sumatran and Ethiopian.
- you know which restaurant serves the freshest arugula.
- a really great parking space can totally move you to tears.

Joke Overheard While High in the Forest

Two tall trees are growing in the forest. A small tree begins to grow between them.

One tall tree says to the other, "Is that a son of a beech or a son of a birch?"

The other tall tree says that it cannot tell. Then a woodpecker lands on the small tree.

"Woodpecker, you are a tree expert," says one tall tree. "Can you tell if that is a son of a beech or a son of a birch?"

The woodpecker takes a taste of the small tree and says, "It is neither a son of a beech nor a son of a birch. That, my tree friends, is the best piece of ash I have ever had the fortune of putting my pecker in."

Q: *How do you get a one-armed hippie out of a tree?*

A: *Pass him a joint.*

A Hastings prostitute is quite impressed when her Chinese client takes her up to his room in the swanky Shangri-La Hotel, where naturally they screw for a while, until he rolls off, gasping for breath.

"Pardon me, I am tired," he explains and goes into the bathroom to freshen up.

When he returns, she is even more impressed by a second round of energetic sex. After a while, though, he lies back on the bed, sighing, "Pardon me, I am tired."

Off he goes to the bathroom again, and again returns ready for another round of vigorous sex.

Q: *What did the hunter get from sitting on the ice too long?*

A: *Polaroids.*

After the sixth session, the prostitute is so tired that

she excuses herself to the bathroom to clean up. When she pulls back the shower curtain, she finds five Chinese guys standing naked in the tub.

Vancouver Bound

Passengers are waiting to board an Air Canada flight to Vancouver when it is announced that the flight is full. The airline is looking for volunteers to give up their seats. In exchange, they'll be given a $100 voucher for their next flight and a first-class seat on the plane leaving an hour later. Eight people run up to the counter to take advantage of the offer.

About 15 seconds later, all eight people sit down grumpily as the lady behind the counter announces, "If there is anyone else *other* than the flight crew who'd like to volunteer, please step forward...."

A wife is holding a lavish dinner party at her beautiful ocean-side home and invites the cream of Vancouver society to attend. To ensure that she is serving only the freshest food at the party, she sends her husband down to the beach to fetch some snails. But while he is collecting, he meets a beautiful woman. Well, one thing leads to another, and they end up going back to her place, drinking wine and making sweet love.

Her husband is so smitten with this woman that he completely loses track of time, and he wakes up the next day in the woman's apartment and realizes what he has done. "My God! I forgot about the party," he says. He gets dressed and runs back to his house just as the sun is rising. Being in a hurry, as he reaches the top of the stairs, he trips and drops his bucket of snails all over the steps. Just then, his wife opens the door with a furious look on her face and says, "Where have you been all night?"

Motto of Salt Spring Island: Save water—shower with a friend.

He looks at her then at the trail of snails and says, "COME ON guys, we are almost there!"

The Death of a Hippie

Two BC lovers who are interested in spiritualism and reincarnation promise each other that if either dies, the survivor will try to contact them from the netherworld in exactly 30 days. Well, a few weeks after making this pact, the young man dies in a car crash. Thirty days later, his sweetheart tries to contact him in a séance.

"Can you hear me, Moonbeam?" she calls out.

A voice calls back instantly. "Yes, Starchild, I hear you. This is Moonbeam."

"Oh, Moonbeam, I miss you so much. What is it like where you are?" she says.

"It's is the most beautiful place, Starchild. There are clear blue skies, a warm breeze and glorious sunshine," says the voice of Moonbeam.

"What do you do all day, my love?"

"Well, Starchild, we are up everyday before sunrise, we eat a plentiful breakfast, then it's nothing but sex until noon. After lunch, we sleep until two, then have sex until five. After dinner, it's more sex, then bed at sundown."

"Moonbeam, is that really what heaven is like?"

"Heaven? I'm not in heaven. I'm a rabbit living on the prairies."

On the Beach

Two Vancouver guys are in a locker room when one guy notices the other guy has a cork in his ass.

He says, "How'd you get a cork stuck in your ass?"

The other guy says, "I was walking along the beach and I tripped over a lamp. There was a puff of smoke, and then a red man in a turban came oozing out. He said, 'I Tonto, Indian Genie. I grant-um one wish.' And I said, 'No sh*t.'"

An Asian lady lives with her English husband in Victoria. The poor lady is not proficient in English but manages to communicate with her husband. The real problem arises whenever she has to shop for groceries.

One day, she goes to the butcher to buy pork legs. She doesn't know how to put forward her request and, in desperation, lifts up her skirt to show her thighs. The butcher gets the message, and the lady goes home with pork legs.

The next day, she needs to get chicken breasts. Again, she doesn't know how to say it, and so she unbuttons her blouse to show the butcher her breasts. The lady gets what she wants.

The third day, the poor lady needs to buy sausages. Unable to find a way to communicate this, she brings her husband to the store and...

What are you thinking?

Hellooooooooooo, her husband speaks English!!

Panda Crimes

Chin-Chin the panda is on trial for entering a Vancouver restaurant, eating dinner, pulling out a machine gun and shooting out the windows and doors.

The judge looks at Chin-Chin's lawyer and proclaims, "Thirty eyewitnesses saw your client pay for dinner, shoot up the place and leave. Security cameras caught the entire incident on video. I have no choice but to sentence your client..."

"Wait a second, your Honour," says the lawyer. "My client may be guilty, but there are extenuating circumstances. He couldn't help his behaviour that night, and if you look up the word 'panda' in the dictionary, you'll have no choice but to agree."

The judge is puzzled, but he has his secretary bring a dictionary into court. There, under the letter "P," he finds, "Panda: black-and-white bear from China that eats shoots and leaves."

A Unique Timepiece

A tour bus in Egypt stops in the middle of a town square. The Kelowna tourists are all shopping at the little stands surrounding the square. One tourist looks at his watch, but it is broken, so he leans over to a local, who is squatting down next to his camel, and asks, "What time is it, sir?"

The local reaches out, softly cups the camel's genitals in his hand and raises them up and down. "It's about 2:00 PM," he says.

The tourist can't believe what he just saw. He runs back to the bus, and sure enough, it is 2:00 PM. He tells a few of the fellow tourists his story. "The man can tell the time by the weight of the camel's genitals!"

One of the doubting tourists walks back to the local and asks him the time. The local again cups and lifts the camel's genitals, then tells the tourist that is 2:05 PM.

The tourist runs back to the bus to tell the story. Finally, the bus driver wants to know how it is done. He walks over and asks the local how he can tell the time from the camel's genitals. The local says, "Sit down here and grab the camel's genitals. Now, lift them up in the air. Now, look underneath them to the other side of the courtyard, where that clock is hanging on the wall."

A yuppie couple from Vancouver decide go to northern BC for a romantic weekend. When they get to the cabin, it is cold so that the wife asks her husband to go chop some wood for the fireplace. He comes in after five minutes and tells his wife that his hands are cold, so she tells him to put his hands between her thighs to warm them.

He does so and goes back outside to finish chopping wood. He comes in after another five minutes and says, "Honey, my hands are cold again." She tells him to put his hands between her thighs to warm them.

He does and then goes back out to chop some more wood. Five minutes pass, and he goes inside again and says, "Honey, my hands are cold again."

> "A Canadian is someone who knows how to make love in a canoe."
>
> –Pierre Berton

She then says, "Damn, don't your ears ever get cold?"

Golf Medic

Two women are playing golf at a Victoria golf club. One tees off and watches with horror as her ball heads directly toward a foursome of men playing the next hole.

The ball hits one of the men, and he immediately falls to the ground, clutching his hands to his groin and rolling around in obvious agony.

The woman rushes over and immediately begins to apologize. "Please allow me to help. I'm a physiotherapist, and I know I can relieve your pain if you'll let me," she tells him.

"Oh no, I'll be all right. I'll be fine in a few minutes," the man replies, still lying in the fetal position, clasping his hands together at his groin.

She is persistent, however, and he finally allows her to help.

She gently takes his hands away, lays them at his sides and then loosens his trousers and puts her hand inside. She administers a tender and skilful massage for several long moments and then asks, "How does that feel?"

He replies, "It feels fabulous, but my thumb still hurts like hell."

Two guys from Smithers are sittin' in a boat on Tyhee Lake, fishing and sucking down beer when all of a sudden Bill says, "I think I'm going to divorce my wife—she hasn't spoken to me in over six months."

Earl sips his beer and says, "You better think it over. Women like that are hard to find."

Age Limit

An ultra-religious man who lives in the BC interior has reached the age of 105 and suddenly stops going to church. Alarmed by the old fellow's absence after so many years of faithful attendance, the priest goes to see him.

He finds the man in excellent health, so the priest asks, "How come after all these years we don't see you at services anymore?"

The old man looks around and lowers his voice. "I'll tell you, father," he whispers. "When I got to be 90, I expected God to take me any day. But then I got to be 95, then 100, then 105. So I figured that God is very busy and must've forgotten about me, and I don't want to remind Him!"

Construction Site

An Italian, an Irishman and a Chinese fellow are hired at a Vancouver construction site. The foreman points to a huge pile of sand and says to the Italian guy, "You're in charge of sweeping."

To the Irishman, he says, "You're in charge of shovelling."

To the Chinese guy, "You're in charge of supplies."

He then says, "Now, I have to leave for a little while. I expect you guys to make a dent in that pile."

So the foreman goes away for a couple hours, but when he returns, the pile of sand is untouched.

He says to the Italian, "Why didn't you sweep any of it?"

The Italian replies in a heavy accent, "I no gotta broom, an' you tella me dat de Chinese'a guy supposa bringa da supplies, but he disappear and I no finda him."

Then the foreman turns to the Irishman and asks why he didn't shovel.

The Irishman replies in his heavy brogue, "Aye, I couldn't get meself a shovel. Ye left the Chinese fella in charge of supplies, but I couldn't fin' him."

The foreman is really angry now and storms off looking for the Chinese guy.

He can't find him anywhere and is getting angrier by the minute. Just then, the Chinese guy springs out from behind the pile of sand and yells, "Supplies!!"

Pulled Over

A Vernon woman is pulled over by police. It goes as follows:

Woman: "Is there a problem, officer?"

Officer: "Ma'am, you were speeding."

Woman: "Oh, I see."

Officer: "Can I see your licence, please?"

Woman: "I'd give it to you, but I don't have one."

Officer: "Don't have one?"

Woman: "Lost it four times for drunk driving."

Officer: "I see...Can I see your vehicle registration papers, please."

Woman: "I can't do that."

Officer: "Why not"?

Woman: "I stole this car."

Officer: "Stole it?"

Woman: "Yes, and I killed and hacked up the owner."

Officer: "You what?"

Woman: "His body parts are in plastic bags in the trunk if you want to see."

The officer looks at the woman, slowly backs away to his car and calls for back-up. Within minutes, five police cruisers circle the car. A senior officer slowly approaches the car, clasping his half-drawn gun.

Officer 2: "Ma'am, could you step out of your vehicle, please!"

The woman steps out of her vehicle.

Woman: "Is there a problem, sir?"

Officer 2: "One of my officers told me that you have stolen this car and murdered the owner.

Woman: "Murdered the owner?

Officer 2: "Yes, could you please open the trunk of your car." The woman opens the trunk, revealing nothing but an empty trunk.

Officer 2: "Is this your car, ma'am?"

Woman: "Yes, here are the registration papers." The first officer is stunned.

Officer 2: "One of my officers claims that you do not have a driver's licence.

The woman digs into her handbag and pulls out a clutch purse and hands it to the officer. The officer snaps open the purse and examines the licence. He looks quite puzzled.

Officer 2: "Thank you ma'am. One of my officers told me you didn't have a licence, that you stole this car and that you murdered and hacked up the owner."

Woman: "Betcha the lying bastard told you I was speeding, too!"

A woman skiing in Whistler complains to her husband that she is in dire need of a restroom. He tells her not to worry, that he is sure there is relief waiting at the top of the lift in the form of a powder room for female skiers in distress. He is wrong, of course, and there is no relief to be found.

The husband, picking up on the intensity of her discomfort, suggests that because she is wearing an all-white ski outfit, she should go off in the woods. No one will even notice, he assures her. The white will provide more than adequate camouflage. So she heads for the tree line, begins disrobing and does her thing.

If you've ever parked on the side of a slope, then you know there is a right way and wrong way to set up your skis so you don't move. Yup, you got it. She positions them the wrong way.

Without warning, the woman finds herself skiing backward out of control, racing through the trees, somehow missing all of them, and onto another slope. Her back side is still bare, her pants down around her knees, and she is picking up speed all the while.

She continues on down the hill, totally out of control, creating an unusual vista for other skiers. The woman "skis" back under the lift and finally collides violently with a pylon. The bad news is that she breaks her arm and is unable to pull up her ski pants. At long last her husband arrives and pulls up her pants, then heads to the base of the mountain and summons the ski patrol, who transports her to a hospital.

She is regrouping in the emergency room when a man with a broken leg is put in the bed next to hers.

"So. How did you break your leg?" she asks, making small talk.

"It was the darndest thing you ever saw," he says. "I was riding up the ski lift, and suddenly I couldn't believe my eyes. Some crazy woman was skiing backward, out of control down the mountain with her bare bottom hanging out of her clothes and pants down around her knees. I leaned over to get a better look, and I guess I didn't realize how far I'd moved. I fell out of the lift. How did you break your arm?"

Business

As I sit in the airport VIP lounge en route to Vancouver, I notice Bill Gates sitting comfortably in the corner, enjoying a drink. I am meeting an important client who is also flying to Vancouver, but she is running a little bit late. Well, being a straightforward kind of guy, I approach the

Microsoft chairman, introduce myself and say, "Mr. Gates, I wonder if you would do me a favour."

"Yes?"

"I'm sitting right over there," I say, pointing to my seat at the bar, "and I'm waiting on a very important client. Would you be so kind when she arrives as to walk by and just say, 'Hi, Mark.'"

"Sure."

I shake his hand, thank him and head back to my seat.

About 10 minutes later, my client shows up. We order a drink and start talking business. A couple of minutes later, I feel a tap on my shoulder. It's Bill Gates.

"Hi, Mark," he says.

I reply, "Get lost, Gates. I'm in a meeting."

The client is impressed.

Smart Dog

In Vernon, a guy sees a sign in front of a house: "Talking Dog for Sale." He rings the bell, and the owner tells him the dog is in the backyard. The guy goes into the backyard and sees a black mutt sitting there.

"You talk?" he asks.

"Sure do."

"So, what's your story?"

The dog looks up and says, "Well, I discovered my gift of speech pretty young, and I wanted to help the government, so I told the CIA. In no time, they had me jetting from country to country, sitting in rooms with spies and world leaders because no one figured a dog would be eavesdropping. I was one of their most valuable spies eight years running."

"But the jetting around really tired me out. I knew I wasn't getting any younger, and I wanted to settle down. So I signed up for a job at the airport to do some undercover security work, mostly wandering near suspicious characters and listening in. I uncovered some incredible dealings there and was awarded a batch of medals."

"After that I had a wife, a mess of puppies, and now I'm just retired."

The guy is amazed. He goes back in and asks the owner what he wants for the dog.

The owner says, "Ten dollars."

"This dog is amazing. Why on Earth are you selling him so cheaply?"

"'Cause he's a liar. He didn't do any of that stuff!"

Racial Discord

A plane leaves Vancouver's airport under the control of a Jewish captain. His copilot is Chinese. It's the first time they've flown together, and an awkward silence between the two seems to indicate a mutual dislike.

Once they reach cruising altitude, the Jewish captain activates the autopilot, leans back in his seat and mutters, "I don't like the Chinese."

"No rike Chinese?" asks the copilot. "Why not?"

"You people bombed Pearl Harbor, that's why!"

"No, no," the copilot protests. "Chinese not bomb Peahl Hahbah! That Japanese, not Chinese."

"Japanese, Chinese, Vietnamese...doesn't matter, you're all alike!" There's a few minutes of silence.

"I no rike Jews either!" the copilot suddenly announces.

"Oh yeah, why not?" asks the captain.

"Jews sink *Titanic*."

"What? That's insane! Jews didn't sink the *Titanic*!" exclaims the captain. "It was an iceberg!"

"Iceberg, Goldberg, Greenberg, Rosenberg...no mattah, all same."

A Vancouver city slicker named Tommy is on vacation in Calgary. His hosts, being very hospitable, invite him to the local rodeo to see the greatest bucking bronco of all time, Blue Steel.

Blue Steel is renowned throughout Alberta for being the toughest, meanest horse there ever was. He has seen off so many would-be riders that the rodeo organizers are promising $10,000 for anyone who can ride him for just 10 seconds.

That afternoon, all the local cowboys try their best, but Blue Steel lives up to his reputation and throws them all off with the greatest of ease.

As a joke, the organizers then offer the prize to anyone in the crowd who dares to tangle with such a beast. Up jumps Tommy and, of course, everyone laughs at him. But the organizers decide to let the city boy have a try.

Blue Steel bucks and lunges, but Tommy not only stays on the horse for 10 seconds, he stays on for 20 seconds, then 30, then a minute! After a few minutes more, Blue Steel is so exhausted that he calms down and Tommy rides him around the ring like a birthday party pony.

Everyone is astonished.

"Considering you've never even sat on a horse before," say Tommy's friends, "how on Earth did you manage that?"

"Easy," says Tommy, "my wife's an epileptic."

Pure Blood

On a train through the Rockies, a Canadian tells off the Englishman sitting across from him in the compartment.

"You English are too stuffy. You set yourselves apart too much. Look at me...in me, I have Italian blood, French blood, a little Indian blood and some Swedish blood. What do you say to that?"

The Englishman says, "Very sporting of your mother."

Kiss and Tell

According to a news report, a certain private school in Surrey is facing a unique problem. A number of 12-year-old girls who are beginning to use lipstick put it on in the bathroom, which would be fine except that after they put on their lipstick, they press their lips to the mirror, leaving dozens of little lip prints.

Every night the maintenance man removes the marks, and the next day the girls put them back.

Finally the principal decides that something has to be done. She calls all the girls to the bathroom and meets them there with the maintenance man. She explains that the lip prints are causing a major problem for the custodian, who has to clean the mirrors every night (you can just imagine the yawns from the little princesses).

She then asks the maintenance man to show the girls how difficult it is to clean the mirrors. He takes out a long-handled squeegee, dips it in the toilet and cleans the mirror with it.

Lip prints no longer appear on the mirror.

A certain religious UBC professor is notorious for getting off topic during lectures and on to his favourite subject: the evils of marijuana.

Off he goes one day into his inventory of horrors. "Used regularly," he explains, "pot can cause psychic disorientation, sterility, cancer and castration!"

"Now wait a minute, Professor," interrupts a student. "Castration? That's absurd!"

"Yes, young man, it's sadly true," replies the professor smugly. "Just suppose your girlfriend gets the munchies!"

Lamaze

A Victoria couple just starting their Lamaze class are given an activity requiring the husband to wear a bag of sand to give him an idea of what it feels like to be pregnant. The husband stands up and shrugs saying, "This doesn't feel so bad."

The instructor then drops a pen and asks the husband to pick it up.

"You want me to pick up the pen as if I were pregnant, the way my wife would do it?" the husband asks.

"Exactly," replies the instructor.

To the delight of the other husbands, he turns to his wife and says, "Honey, pick up that pen for me."

An elderly man in Kelowna owns a large farm with a large pond in the back, picnic tables, horseshoe courts and some apple and peach trees. The pond is properly shaped and fixed up for swimming. One evening the old farmer decides to go down to the pond and look it over because he hadn't been there for a while. He grabs a 20-litre bucket to bring back some fruit. As he nears the pond, he hears voices shouting and laughing with glee. As he gets closer, he sees a bunch of young women skinny-dipping in his pond. He makes the women aware of his presence, and they all go to the deep end.

One of the women shouts to him, "We're not coming out until you leave!"

The old man frowns. "I didn't come down here to watch you ladies swim naked or make you get out of the pond naked," he says. He holds up the bucket. "I'm here to feed the alligator."

The owner of a golf course on Vancouver Island is confused about paying an invoice, so he decides to ask his secretary for some mathematical help.

He calls her into his office and says, "You graduated from the University of British Columbia, and I need some help. If I were to give you $20,000, minus 14 percent, how much would you take off?"

The secretary thinks for a moment then replies, "Everything but my earrings."

Proper Manners

Three men are using the urinals in a public restroom in the UK. The first man finishes relieving himself, zips up, strolls to the sinks and washes his hands, using plenty of soap and water and doing a splendidly thorough job. As he is drying his hands (with lots of paper towels), he loftily announces to no one in particular: "At Oxford, I learned to be clean and sanitary." The man then leaves the bathroom in a cloud of self-satisfaction.

The second gent zips up, marches briskly to the sinks and scrubs his hands with much less soap and water than the first man, doing a splendidly thorough job nonetheless. As he dries his hands (with only one paper towel), he announces to no one in particular, "At Cambridge, I learned to be clean and sanitary, but I *also* learned to be thrifty and environmentally conscious." He then strides from the bathroom with a purposeful air.

The third man finishes relieving himself, zips up and ambles past the sinks to the door, muttering to himself: "In British Columbia, we learn to not piss on our hands."

A BC man, a Russian man and an African man are all up in a hot air balloon together. After a few minutes, the Russian man puts his hand down through the clouds. "Aaah!" he says. "We're right over my homeland."

"How can you tell?" asks the Canadian.

"I can feel the cold air," he replies.

A few hours later, the African man puts his hand through the clouds. "Aaah! We're right over my homeland," he says.

"How do you know that?" asks the Russian.

"I can feel the heat of the desert."

Several more hours later, the Canadian puts his hand through the clouds. "Aaah! We're right over Vancouver. Right over East Hastings, to be exact."

The Russian and the African are amazed. "How do you know that?" they exclaim.

The BC man pulls his hand up. "My watch is missing."

Chapter Seven

The True North

In the North, it is Sooooo Cold that...

- we can't eat with metal cutlery—some people walk around for days with spoons or forks stuck to their tongues.
- hitchhikers hold up pictures of thumbs.
- when I dial 911, a recorded message says to phone back in spring.
- the optician gives away free ice scrapers with every new pair of eyeglasses.
- pickpockets stick their hands in strangers' pockets just to keep them warm.
- squirrels in the park throw themselves at an electric fence.
- I chipped a tooth on my soup.
- Grandpa's teeth are chattering—in the glass.
- words freeze in the air—if you want to hear what someone said, you have to grab a handful of sentences and warm them by the fire.
- down at the city morgue, you can't tell the stiffs from the guys who work there.
- Shania Twain covers her midriff.
- refrigerators are redundant.
- the local flasher describes himself to women.
- my balls have become ovaries.
- the hookers downtown charge 20 bucks just to blow on your hands.

How Cold is It?

Three Inuit at their local Yukon bar get to talking about how cold it is outside and how cold their igloos are. Each believes they have the coldest igloo, so they leave the bar to determine who is correct.

Q: Where do seals go to see a movie?

A: The dive-in.

They go to the first guy's igloo, where he says, "Watch this!" and pours a cup of water into the air. The water freezes in mid-air and falls to the floor in a solid chunk.

"Not bad," the others say, but each maintains that their igloo is colder still.

So they go to the second guy's igloo, and he says, "Watch this!" and takes a big breath and exhales, whereupon his breath freezes into a big lump and falls to the floor.

"Wow, that's colder than mine!" says the first guy.

But the third man claims his igloo is colder still. So they go to the third Inuit's igloo.

He says, "Watch this!" and goes into the bedroom, throws back the thick furs and retrieves one of several small balls of ice. He takes it, puts it on a spoon and holds a match under it.

When it's heated up enough, it goes, "FFFAAAARRRRTTT."

Riding the Tundra

A guy is riding across the tundra on his snowmobile when his vehicle starts sputtering. He cruises into town and stops at a mechanic's shop. After 5 or 10 minutes, the mechanic returns and says, "Looks like you just blew a seal."

"No, I haven't. That's just frost on my moustache!"

A tourist goes to the North Pole and meets an Inuit. "During the summer, you don't have any nights, and during the winter, you don't have any days...what do you do during those endless summer days?" he asks.

"We go fishing and make love to our women," the Inuit replies.

The tourist thinks for a while and asks, "Then what do you do during those endless winter nights?"

The Inuit grins and says, "We don't go fishing."

Two Guys from the Yukon

First guy: "Where does your mother come from?"

Second guy: "Alaska."

First guy: "Don't bother, I'll ask her myself!"

Q: *What do you call a lesbian from Yellowknife?*

A: *A Klon-dike.*

Convention Argument

Two Inuit surgeons are arguing during a medical convention.

"No," says one surgeon. "I tell you, it is 'woomba.'"

The other, equally sure, says, "And I am telling you, it is 'whoooommmm.'"

After 10 minutes of this, a surgeon from Toronto interrupts. "Excuse me, gentlemen, but I think the word you're looking for is 'womb.'"

The Toronto surgeon walks away, pleased with himself. The two Inuit surgeons turn to each other and one says, "I bet he has never even seen an elephant seal, never mind heard one fart underwater."

In the North, it takes six months to teach children the difference between day and night

An Inuk asks a local priest, "If I did not know about God and sin, would I still go to hell?"

"No," says the priest, "not if you did not know."

The Inuk replies, "Then why the heck did you tell me?"

Yukon Warning

In light of the rising frequency of human–grizzly bear conflicts, the Yukon division of Parks Canada advises hikers, hunters and fishermen to take extra precautions and keep alert for bears while in the field.

"We advise that outdoorsmen wear noisy little bells on their clothing so as not to startle bears that aren't expecting them. We also advise outdoorsmen to carry pepper spray with them in case of an encounter with a bear. It is also a good idea to watch out for fresh signs of bear activity. Outdoorsmen should recognize the difference between black bear and grizzly bear droppings: black bear droppings are smaller and contain lots of berries and squirrel fur, whereas grizzly bear droppings have little bells in them and smell like pepper."

> **Q:** *What does an Inuit use to keep his house together?*
>
> **A:** *Iglue.*

A guy from Yellowknife is walking down the street with a case of beer under his arm.

His friend Doug stops him and asks, "Hey Bob! Whatcha get the case of beer for?"

"I got it for my wife, eh," answers Bob.

"Oh!" exclaims Doug. "Good trade."

Not a City Boy

A young guy at a bar in Dawson City, Yukon, notices two girls deep in conversation. He walks over and asks, "You girls want a drink?"

Q: What do snowmen wear on their heads?

A: Icecaps

"You're wasting your time," says one of the ladies. "We're lesbians."

"What's a lesbian?" he asks.

"We like to have sex with girls," she replies.

"Hey there!" the guy calls to the bartender. "Three drinks over here for us lesbians, please."

Two Inuit men out on a long hunt sit in a kayak. They are really cold, so they light a fire in the kayak. Naturally, it sinks. This proves that you can't have your kayak and heat it, too.

A Warm Scene

Outside, as a winter storm raged, an Inuit mother sits in her warm igloo holding her little boy in her arms while reading nursery rhymes.

"Little Jack Horner sat in a corner eating his curds..."

"Mother, mother," interrupts the boy. "What's a corner?"

In a courtroom in Inuvik, Northwest Territories, a man suspected of murder is hauled in before the court.

"Court is now in session," says the judge. "The Crown Attorney may proceed with questioning the defendant."

The Crown Attorney puffs up his chest and says, "Where were you on the night of October 3 to December 16?"

It is so cold in Inuvik that residents go south to Edmonton in the winter to get away from it all.

Chase Me

A couple of Yukon boys are fishing at their special pond off the beaten track. All of a sudden, a park ranger jumps out of the bushes. Immediately, one of the boys throws his rod down and starts running through the woods like a bat out of hell. The park ranger is hot on his heels.

After about a kilometre, the young man stops and rests with his hands on his thighs to catch his breath, letting the park ranger catch up to him.

"Let's see your fishing licence, boy!" the ranger gasps.

The boy pulls out his wallet and gives the ranger his valid fishing licence.

"Well, son," says the park ranger. "You must be about as dumb as a box of rocks!

> **Q:** *Why do Northerners buy refrigerators?*
>
> **A:** *To keep their food from freezing.*

You don't have to run from me if you have a valid licence!"

"Yes, sir," replies the young guy. "But my friend back there, well, he don't have one."

Death of a Virgin

In a tiny village on the James Bay coast lives an old lady, a virgin and proud of it. Sensing that her final days are rapidly approaching and wanting to make sure everything is in proper order when she dies, she goes to the town's undertaker—who also happens to be the local postal clerk—to make the proper arrangements.

As a last wish, she informs the undertaker that she wants the following inscription engraved on her tombstone: BORN A VIRGIN, LIVED A VIRGIN, DIED A VIRGIN.

Q: What is the Inuit word for "lousy hunter"?

A: Vegetarian.

Not long after, the old maid dies peacefully. A few days after the funeral, as the undertaker/postal clerk goes to prepare the tombstone the lady requested, it becomes quite apparent that the tombstone she selected is much too small for the wording she chose. He thinks long and hard about how he can fulfill the old maid's final request, considering the very limited space available on the small piece of stone.

For days, he agonizes over the dilemma. But finally his experience as a postal worker enables him to come up with what he thinks is the appropriate solution to the problem.

The virgin's tombstone is engraved, and it read as follows: RETURNED UNOPENED.

A Northern Cree boy goes to his mother one day with a puzzled look on his face. "Say, Mom, why is my bigger brother named Mighty Storm?"

"Because he was conceived during a mighty storm," she says.

Then he asks, "Why is my sister named Cornflower?"

"Well, your father and I were in a cornfield when we made her," she replies.

He then asks, "And why is my other sister called Moonchild?"

"We were watching the moon landing when she was conceived," the mother replies.

The mother paused and said to her son, "Tell me, Torn Rubber, why are you so curious?"

Back Woods Folk

Deep in the woods of the Yukon, a man's wife goes into labour in the middle of the night, and the doctor is called out to assist in the delivery. Because there is no electricity, the doctor hands the father-to-be a lantern and says, "Here, you hold this high so I can see what I'm doing." Soon, a baby boy is brought into the world. "Whoa there," says the doctor. "Don't be in a rush to put the lantern down...I think there's yet another one to come."

Sure enough, within minutes, he also delivers a baby girl. "No, no, don't be in a great hurry to put down that lantern...It seems there's yet another one in there!" says the doctor.

The husband scratches his head in bewilderment and asks the doctor, "Do you think it's the light that's attracting them?"

Reindeer Games

According to the Northwest Territories Department of Fish and Game, while both male and female reindeer grow antlers in the summer each year, male reindeer drop their antlers at the beginning of winter, usually late November to mid-December. Female reindeer retain their antlers until after they give birth in spring. Therefore, according to historical renditions depicting Santa's reindeer, every single one of them, from Rudolph to Blitzen, has to be a girl.

We should have known. Only women would be able to drag a fat man in a red velvet suit all around the world in one night and not get lost!

A local man is found murdered in his home in Whitehorse. Detectives at the scene find the man face down in his bathtub. The tub has been filled with milk and corn flakes, and the deceased has a banana protruding from his buttocks.

Police suspect a cereal killer.

Torture

A young man is wandering in a forest in the Northwest Territories when he comes upon a small house. He knocks on the door and is greeted by an ancient Indian man with a long, grey beard. "I'm lost," says the man. "Can you put me up for the night?"

"Certainly," the Indian man says, "but on one condition. If you so much as lay a finger on my daughter, I will inflict upon you the three worst Indian tortures known to man."

"Okay," says the man, thinking that the daughter must be pretty old as well, and enters the house.

Before dinner, the daughter comes down the stairs. She is young and beautiful with a fantastic figure. She is obviously attracted to the young man and can't keep her eyes off him during the meal. Remembering the old man's warning, he ignores her and goes up to bed alone.

But during the night, he can bear it no longer and sneaks into her room for a night of passion. He is careful to keep everything quiet so the old man won't hear. Near dawn, he creeps back to his room, exhausted, but happy.

He wakes in the morning with the feeling of pressure on his chest. Opening his eyes, he sees a large rock on his chest with a note on it that reads, "Indian Torture 1: Large rock on chest."

"Well, that's pretty crappy," he thinks. "But if that's the best the old man can do, I don't have much to worry about."

He picks the boulder up, walks over to the window and throws the boulder out. As he does so, he notices another note that reads: "Indian Torture 2: Rock tied to left testicle."

In a panic, he glances down and sees the rope, which is already getting close to the end.

Figuring that a few broken bones is better than castration, he jumps out the window after the boulder.

As he plummets downward, he sees a large sign on the ground that reads, "Indian Torture 3: Right testicle tied to bedpost."

A Yukon family is visiting a big city for the first time. The father and son are in the hotel lobby when they spot an elevator.

"What's that, Dad?" the boy asks.

"I never did see nothing like that in my life," replies the father.

Seconds later, an old, frail woman walks in the hotel door and hobbles to the elevator. She presses the button with her cane, waits for the doors to open and gets in.

The father and son, still amazed by this contraption, continue to watch.

They hear a ping noise, and the doors open again. Out steps a beautiful 20-year-old busty blonde.

The father looks at his son and says, "Go get your mother!"

Fishing Secrets

A man is ice fishing on the frozen banks of James Bay and not having much luck at all. A small boy comes along, bores a hole in the ice not too far away and starts fishing as well.

"Good luck," says the man. "They ain't biting today."

But after a few minutes, the boy catches a humongous fish. A few minutes later, he pulls another out, then another and another. Meanwhile, the man hasn't had a bite.

Wanting to know his secret, the man goes over to the boy, "Hey sonny, what's your secret? I've been out here all day in this darn cold, and I haven't even had a bite. What are you doing that I ain't?"

The boy replies, "Yu haft u kip yr wrms wrm."

"What was that?" says the man.

The boy spits into a bucket, "I said, 'You have to keep your worms warm.'"

A drunken resident of Whitehorse decides that he wants to go fishing. He packs up all his tackle and sets out in search of a suitable spot. Eventually, he stumbles across a huge area of ice and decides that he'll give it a go. Taking out a saw from his tackle box, he starts to make a hole.

Suddenly, a loud voice booms out at him, "There's no fish in here."

The drunk looks all around him but can't see anyone. He decides it's just the booze talking and carries on sawing.

Again, the voice booms out, "I've told you once, there's no fish in here!"

He looks up again, but there's still no sign of anyone, so he returns to sawing the ice.

"Stop it!" shouts a now very angry voice. "You'd better pack up your stuff and get out of here or there'll be trouble."

"Who are you?" shouts the drunk. "Are you God?"

"I'm the manager of this ice rink!"

A nun, a priest, an Irishman, a Jew, a Newfie, a rabbi and an Eskimo walk into a bar.

The bartender looks at them and asks, "Is this some kind of joke?"

Train Ride

Two Inuit guys are taking their first trip on the train. A vendor comes down the corridor selling bananas, which they'd never seen before. Each buys one.

The first man eagerly peels the banana and bites into it just as the train goes into a tunnel. When the train emerges from the tunnel, he looks across to his friend and says, "I wouldn't eat that if I were you."

"Why not?"

"I took one bite and went blind for half a minute."

Leaving Yellowknife

When it's wintertime in Yellowknife
The gentle breezes blow,
About 100 kilometres per hour
And it's 52 below.

You can tell you're in Yellowknife,
'Cause the snow's up to your butt,
And you take a breath of winter air
And your nose holes both freeze shut.

The weather here is wonderful,
So I guess I'll hang around;
I could never leave Yellowknife now,
My feet are frozen to the ground.

The Polar Bear?

A young polar bear comes into his den and asks his mother, "Mom, am I a real polar bear?"

"Of course you are," his mother replies.

The young polar bear asks his father, "Dad, am I a real polar bear?"

"Yes, you are a real polar bear."

A week passes, and the young polar bear asks his parents, "Are grandma and grandpa real polar bears?"

"Yes," say his parents.

Another week passes, and the young polar bear asks his parents, "Are all my relatives real polar bears?"

"Yes, they are all real polar bears. Why do you ask?"

"Because," says the young polar bear. "I'm freezing!"

It is a fact that all polar bears are left-handed. I want to meet the scientist who gave them the pens.

Joe grew up in Whitehorse, then moved away to attend college and law school, but he now decides to move back to Whitehorse because he believes he can be a big shot at home. He really wants to impress everyone, so he returns and opens a new law office.

The first day, he sees a man coming up the passageway and decides to make a big impression on this potential client. As the man comes to the door, Joe picks up the phone. He motions the man in, all the while talking. "No. Absolutely not. You tell those clowns in Calgary that I won't settle this case for less than one million. Yes, the Court of Appeal has agreed to hear that case next week. I'll be handling the primary argument, and the other members of my team will provide support. Okay, tell the District Attorney that I'll meet with him next week to discuss the details."

> "I don't trust any country that looks around a continent and says, 'Hey, I'll take the frozen part.'"
>
> –Jon Stewart

The "conversation" goes on for almost five minutes. All the while, the man sits patiently as Joe rattles off instructions. Finally, Joe puts down the phone and turns to the man. "I'm sorry for the delay, but as you can see, I'm very busy. What can I do for you?"

The man replies, "I'm from Bell, the telephone company. I'm here to hook up your phone."

CHAPTER EIGHT

Political Leanings

On a Plane

Pauline Marois, Thomas Mulcair and Stephen Harper are on a private jet together. Stephen Harper gets an idea. He says, "I'm gonna throw this $100 bill out the window and make one Canadian really really happy."

Pauline Marois doesn't want to be outdone, so she says, "I trow dese two $50 bills out the window and make two Québecois peoples really really happy."

Q: Why did the Canadian cross the road?

A: To get in the middle.

Thomas Mulcair decides to go with the flow and says, "I'll throw these 100 loonies out the window and make 100 Canadians really, really happy."

At this point, the pilot comes through the door and says, "If you three don't shut the hell up right now, I'll throw all three of you out the window and make 35 million Canadians really, really happy."

A Canadian voter dies and goes to heaven. As he stands in front of St. Peter at the Pearly Gates, he sees a huge wall of clocks behind him. "What are all those clocks?" he asks.

St. Peter answers, "Those are Lie-Clocks. Everyone on Earth has a Lie-Clock. Every time you lie, the hands on your clock move."

Q: How do you annoy a Conservative?

A: Vote.

"Oh," says the man. "Whose clock is that?"

"That's Jack Layton's. The hands have never moved, indicating that he's never told a lie."

"Incredible," says the man. "And whose clock is that one?"

St. Peter responds, "That's Sir John A. Macdonald's clock. The hands have moved twice, telling us that Sir John told only two lies in his entire life."

"Where's Stephen Harper's clock?" asked the man.

"Harper's clock is in Jesus' office. After all the election promises, Jesus uses it as a ceiling fan."

Bus Crash

A bus filled with Ottawa politicians is driving through the Ontario countryside. The bus driver, caught up in the beautiful scenery, loses control and crashes into the ditch. A farmer living nearby hears the horrible crash and rushes out to the wreckage. Finding the Ottawa politicians, he buries them.

Later that day, the Mounties come to the farm to question the man. "So you buried all those politicians?" asks an officer. "Were they all dead?"

The farmer answers, "Some said they weren't, but you know how politicians lie."

Out for a Jog

Prime Minister Stephen Harper is out jogging one morning when he trips, falls over a bridge railing and lands in the Ottawa River.

Before the RCMP can get to him, three kids who are fishing pull him out of the water.

Harper is so grateful that he offers the kids whatever they want.

The first kid says, "I sure would like to go to Canada's Wonderland."

Harper says, "No problem. I'll take you there on my Canadian Government Jet."

The second kid says, "I really need a new baseball glove."

Harper says, "I'll get it for you and even have a Blue Jays pitcher sign it!"

The third kid says, "I want a motorized wheelchair with a built-in TV and stereo headset!"

Harper is a little perplexed by this request and says, "But you don't look like you are injured."

The kid says, "I will be after my dad finds out I saved your Conservative butt from drowning!"

A priest walks into a barbershop in Ottawa. After getting his haircut, he asks how much it costs.

The barber says, "No, charge. I consider it a service to the Lord."

The next morning, the barber arrives for work and finds 12 prayer books and a thank-you note from the priest at his front door.

> **Q:** *Why don't politicians like golf?*
>
> *A: Because it's too much like their work—trapped in one bad lie after another.*

Later in the day, a police officer walks into the same barber shop. After getting his haircut, he asks how much he owes.

The barber replies, "No charge. I consider it a service to the community."

The next morning, the barber arrives for work and finds 12 doughnuts and a thank-you note from the police officer.

Then a senator walks into the barbershop. After getting his haircut, he asks how much owes.

The barber replies, "No charge. I consider it a service to the nation."

The next morning, the barber arrives for work to find 12 senators at the front door.

A Simple Request

A little boy desperately needs $100 to buy a present. His mother suggests that he pray for it, so he writes God a letter asking for the money. The post office intercepts the letter and forwards it to the Prime Minister, who is so touched by the request that he instructs his secretary to send the boy $5.

On receiving the money, the boy writes back, "Dear God, thank you very much for sending me the money. I noticed that you sent it through Ottawa. As usual, those crooks deducted $95."

Fallible God

God made the rivers,
And God made the lakes.
But when God made Stephen Harper,
He made a mistake.

> "I want to thank all the Canadians who came out today to wave to me—with all five fingers!"
>
> –President George W. Bush (during his first visit to Ottawa Nov. 30, 2004)

Little Ralph is in his fifth grade class when the teacher asks the children what their fathers do for a living. One kid says firefighter, another says businessman, etc. Little Ralph is not saying anything, so the teacher asks about his father.

Little Ralph says, "My father is an exotic dancer at a gay bar and takes all his clothes off in front of other men. Sometimes, if the offer is really good, he'll go out into the alley with some guy and have sex with him for money."

Immediately the class begins to laugh. The teacher pulls Little Ralph out of the class and asks, "Is this really true about your father?"

"Well, not really," says Little Ralph. "He is a Member of Parliament, but I was just too embarrassed to say that in front of the other kids."

Alex Trebek will be hosting a new reality show on Canadian television called *Canada's Next Prime Minister*. The show was originally going to be called *The Biggest Hoser*.

Custody Battle

A case regarding the custody of a small child is brought before a judge. The judge asks the boy, "Do you want to live with your mother?"

"No," replies the boy. "I don't want to live with her because she beats me!"

"Do you want to live with your father?" asks the judge.

"No, he beats me too," answers the boy.

Finally the judge says, "Well, where do you want to live?"

"Well," responds the child. "I want to live with the New Democratic Party."

"Why do you want to live with the NDP?"

"Because," exclaims the boy, "the NDP don't beat anybody."

Mirror, Mirror

On a Monday, Syria's president Bashar al-Assad stands before his magic mirror and asks, "Mirror, mirror, on the wall, who is the evilest man in all of Syria?"

"Thou art, my master," replies the magic mirror.

"Good," replies Assad, flashing an evil grin. He then calls his general of the army and barks orders at him. "Go out into the streets of every city, and rape and pillage the people."

On Wednesday, Assad again stands before his magic mirror and says, "Who is the evilest man in all of the Middle East?"

"Thou art, my master," replies the magic mirror.

"Good," replies Assad. Again he summons his general and orders them to go forth into the streets and across the borders and rape and kill everyone in sight.

On Friday, Assad yet again stands before his magic mirror and asks, "Who is the evilest man in all the world?"

Assad listens to the magic mirror, but instead of smiling this time, he begins to turn red with anger. He summons the general and says, "Who is this Stephen Harper?"

Q: *If Stephen Harper and Rona Ambrose were on a sinking ship, who would be saved?*

A: The country.

Pied Piper of Ottawa

A tourist wanders into a back-alley antique shop somewhere in Ottawa. Picking through the objects on display, he discovers a detailed, life-sized bronze sculpture of a rat. The sculpture is so interesting and unique that he picks it up and asks the shop owner what it costs. "Twelve dollars for the rat, sir," says the shop owner, "and a $1000 more for the story behind it."

"You can keep the story, old man," he replies, "but I'll take the rat."

Once the transaction is complete, the tourist leaves the store with the bronze rat under his arm. As he crosses the street, two live rats emerge from a sewer drain and fall into step behind him. Nervously looking over his shoulder, he begins to walk faster, but every time he passes another sewer drain, more rats come out and follow him. By the time he's walked two blocks, at least a hundred rats are at his heels, and people begin to point and shout. He walks even faster and soon breaks into a trot as multitudes of rats swarm from sewers, basements, vacant lots and abandoned cars.

Q: *Why did the Tory cross the road?*

A: Because that's where his driver parked the car.

Rats by the thousands are at his heels, and as he sees the waterfront at the bottom of the hill, he panics and starts to run full tilt. No matter how fast he runs, the rats keep up, squealing hideously, now not just thousands but millions, so that by the time he comes rushing up to the water's edge, a trail of rats 12 city blocks long is behind him.

Making a mighty leap, he jumps up onto a light post, grasping it with one arm as he hurls the bronze rat into the Ottawa River as far as he can heave it. Pulling his legs up and clinging to the light post, he watches in amazement as the seething tide of rats surges into the river, where they drown.

Shaken and mumbling, he makes his way back to the antique shop.

"So, you've come back for the rest of the story," says the owner.

"No," says the tourist. "I was wondering if you have a bronze senator."

Q: *What's the difference between senators in the United States and in Canada?*

A: *In the United States, you have to win an election to become a senator. In Canada you have to lose one.*

A Canadian Political Lesson

"Daddy," a little girl asks her father, "do all fairy tales begin with 'Once upon a time?'"

"No, sweetheart," he answers. "Some begin with 'If I am elected....'"

A woman who has been married three times walks into a bridal shop one day and tells the sales clerk that she is looking for a wedding gown for her fourth wedding.

"Of course, madam," replies the sales clerk. "Exactly what type and colour dress are you looking for?"

The bride-to-be says: "A long frilly white dress with a veil."

The sales clerk hesitates a bit, then says, "Please don't take this the wrong way, but gowns of that nature are considered more appropriate for brides who are being married for the first time—for those who are a bit more innocent, if you know what I mean? Perhaps ivory or sky blue would be nice?"

"Well," replies the customer, a little peeved at the clerk's directness. "I can assure you that a white gown would be quite appropriate. Believe it or not, despite all my marriages, I remain as innocent as any first-time bride. You see, my first husband was so excited about our wedding that he died as we were checking into our hotel. My second husband and I got into such a terrible fight in the limo on our way to our honeymoon that we had the wedding annulled immediately and never spoke to each other again."

Q: *Why did the chicken cross the road?*

Vic Toews: *"The chicken did not cross the road. I repeat, the chicken did not cross the road. I don't know any chickens. I have never known any chickens."*

"What about your third husband?" asks the sales clerk.

"That one was a Conservative," says the woman, "and every night for four years, he just sat on the edge of the bed and told me how good it was going to be."

Invasion

Prime Minister Stephen Harper is awakened one night by an urgent call from the Minister of Defence.

"Mr. Harper," says the minister, barely able to contain himself. "There's good news and bad news."

"Oh, no," mutters the Prime Minister. "Well, let me have the bad news first."

"The bad news, sir, is that we've been invaded by creatures from another planet."

"Gosh, and the good news?"

"The good news, sir, is that they eat reporters and piss oil."

A teacher tells her class to make a list of the greatest Canadian politicians. After about 10 minutes, every one finishes the assignment except Little Johnny.

The teacher asks, "Why haven't you finished your list, young man?"

He replies, "I got nothing to write about."

CANADA REVENUE AGENCY'S NEW SIMPLIFIED TAX FORM FOR 2013 TAXES

1. How much money did you make in 2013?
2. Send it to us.

Conservative Economy

Because of the current financial situation caused by the economic slowdown, Parliament has decided to implement a scheme proposed by Stephen Harper to put workers of 55 years of age and above on early, mandatory retirement, thus creating jobs and reducing unemployment. All MPs support it. This scheme will be known as RAPE (Retire Aged People Early).

Persons selected to be RAPEd can apply to Parliament to be considered for the SHAFT (Special Help After Forced Termination) program.

Persons who have been RAPEd and SHAFTed will be reviewed under the SCREW (System Covering Retired-Early Workers) program.

A person may be RAPEd once, SHAFTed twice and SCREWed as many times as Parliament deems appropriate.

Persons who have been RAPEd could get AIDS (Additional Income for Dependents and Spouse) or HERPES (Half Earnings for Retired Personnel Early Severance).

Obviously persons who have AIDS or HERPES will not be SHAFTed or SCREWed any further by Parliament.

Persons who are not RAPEd and are staying on will receive as much SHIT (Special High Intensity Training) as possible. Parliament has always prided itself on the amount of SHIT it gives our citizens.

Should you feel that you do not receive enough SHIT, please bring this to the attention of your MP, who has been trained to give you all the SHIT you can handle.

Sincerely, the committee for Economic Value of Individual Lives (EVIL).

P.S. Thanks to recent budget cuts and the rising cost of electricity, gas and oil, as well as current market conditions, the Light at the End of the Tunnel has been turned OFF.

Nice Politicians

A Conservative and a New Democrat are walking down the street when they come across a homeless person.

The Conservative gives the homeless person his business card and tells him to come to his business for a job. He then takes $20 out of his pocket and gives it to the man.

The New Democrat is impressed, and when they come to another homeless person, he decides to help. He walks over to the homeless person and gives him directions to the welfare office. He then reaches into the Conservative's pocket and gets out $20. He keeps $15 for administrative fees and gives the homeless person $5.

Two friends are discussing politics on election day, each trying to no avail to convince the other to switch sides.

Finally, one says to the other, "Look, it's clear that we are unalterably opposed on every political issue. My Conservative vote and your Liberal vote will surely cancel each other out. Why not save ourselves some time and both agree to not vote today?"

The other agrees enthusiastically, and they part.

Shortly thereafter, a friend of the Conservative who had heard the conversation says, "That was a sporting offer you made."

"Not really," says the Conservative. "This is the third time I've done this today."

Awww Cute!

Stephen Harper and a Canadian Security Intelligence Service agent are taking a stroll in an Ottawa park when they come upon a little girl carrying a basket with a blanket over it. Curious, Harper asks the girl, "What's in the basket?"

"New baby kittens. Their eyes are still shut," she replies and opens the basket to show him.

"How nice," says Harper. "What kind are they?"

The little girl says, "Conservatives."

Harper smiles, pats the little girl on the head and continues on.

Three weeks later, Harper is taking another stroll, this time with Justin Trudeau. They see the little girl again with the same basket.

Harper says, "Watch this, Justin. It's really cute." They approach the little girl. Harper greets her and says "How are the kittens doing?"

"Fine," she replies.

Then, smirking, he nudges Trudeau with his elbow and asks the little girl, "And can you tell us what kind of kittens they are?"

She replies, "Liberals."

Abashed, Harper says, "But three weeks ago you said they were Conservatives!'

"I know," she says. "But now their eyes are open."

A woman in a hot air balloon realizes she is lost. She lowers her altitude and spots a man in a boat below. She shouts to him, "Excuse me, can you help me? I promised a friend I would meet him an hour ago, but I don't know where I am."

The man consults his portable GPS and replies, "You're in a hot air balloon, approximately 10 metres above a ground elevation of 715 metres above sea level. You are at 31 degrees, 14.97 minutes north latitude and 100 degrees, 49.09 minutes west longitude.

She rolls her eyes and says, "You must be a Conservative."

"I am," replies the man. "How did you know?"

"Well," answers the balloonist, "everything you told me is technically correct, but I have no idea what to do with your information, and I'm still lost. Frankly, you've not been much help to me."

The man smiles and responds, "You must be a Liberal."

"I am," replies the balloonist. "How did you know?"

"Well," said the man, "you don't know where you are or where you're going. You've risen to where you are because of a large quantity of hot air. You made a promise that you have no idea how to keep, and you expect me to solve your problem. You're in exactly the same position you were in before we met, but it's now somehow my fault."

The Engineer and the MP

A young engineer is leaving his Ottawa office at 4:45 PM when he sees the federal Member of Parliament from his riding standing in his office in front of a shredder with a piece of paper in his hand.

"Listen," says the MP, "this is a very sensitive and important document, and my secretary is not here. Can you make this thing work?"

"Certainly," says the engineer. He turns the machine on, inserts the paper and presses the start button.

"Excellent, excellent!" says the Member of Parliament as his paper disappears inside the machine. "I just need one copy."

Lesson: Never, never, ever assume that your Member of Parliament knows what he or she is doing.

≪ Chapter Nine ≫

Our Sporting Tradition

It Unites and Divides

Two boys are playing hockey on a pond in a park in Edmonton. One is wearing an Oilers jersey and the other is wearing a plain jersey. As they play, a rabid Rottweiler appears and attacks the boy with the Oilers jersey. Thinking quickly, the other boy takes his stick, wedges it down the dog's collar and twists, breaking the dog's neck and killing it instantly.

A reporter who is strolling by sees the incident and rushes over to interview the boy. "The headline will read 'Young Oilers Fan Saves Friend from Vicious Animal.' You're a hero kid!" says the reporter.

"But I'm not a Oilers fan," the little hero replies.

> **Q:** *Why are the Toronto Maple Leafs like Canada Post?*
>
> **A:** *They both wear uniforms and neither delivers!*

"Sorry. Because we are in Edmonton and your friend is wearing an Oilers jersey, I just figured you were," replies the reporter. "How about this then? 'Little Eskimos Fan Rescues Friend From Horrific Attack.'"

"I'm not a Eskimos fan, either," says the boy.

"I assumed everyone in Edmonton was either an Oilers or Eskimos fan. What team do you root for kid?" asks the reporter.

"Well, I'm a Montréal Canadiens fan," says the little boy.

The reporter's smile changes into a frown and he says, "Well, in that case the new headline will read, 'Little French Bastard Kills Beloved Family Pet.'"

Hockey players complain about the violence in the game and have been for years now. It's just that without any teeth, no one can understand them.

Bragging at Tim Hortons

Four women are having coffee and bragging about their children. The first woman says, "My son is a priest. When he walks into a room, everyone calls him 'Father.'"

The next woman tries to top her, "Really? Well, my son married the princess of a small European country, and when he walks into a room, people call him 'Your Highness.'"

> Did you hear about the change Canada Post made to their stamps? There used to be Leafs players on them, but people did not know what side to spit on.

The third woman chimes in, "Well, my son is a cardinal of the church. Whenever he walks into a room, people call him 'Your Eminence!'"

> **Q:** *What is the difference between a hockey game and a prize-fight?*
>
> **A:** *In a hockey game, the fights are real.*

The fourth woman is just sitting there sipping her coffee silently and confidently. The three other women look at her in a not-so-subtle way, as if to say "well?"

She smiles and says, "Oh, my son is a very large and handsome hockey player. Whenever he walks into a room, women say, 'OH MY GOD!'"

A Canadian In Hell

A passionate hockey fan dies and goes to hell. The Devil appears before him and says, "What do you feel like doing today? You can have anything you like."

Being a hockey lover, he says to the Devil, "Well, I can think of nothing better to do than play a game of hockey. Can we do that?"

"Certainly," says the Devil. With a snap of his fingers, they are in front of the most beautiful arena in the world. They walk in and the place is filled with screaming hockey fans. In the dressing room, the man sees all the past greats of hockey—Eddie Shore, Howie Morenz, Jacques Plante, Maurice Richard—all getting ready to play a game with him. Thinking hell is not as bad as everyone makes it out to be, he gets dressed in the best hockey equipment, puts on the sharpest skates and picks up a golden stick. Out on the ice, he thinks this is the greatest thing in the world. When the referee signals to start the game, he approaches the face-off circle, where the legendary

Joe Malone stands waiting as his opponent. The man stands there waiting for the puck to drop, but nothing happens.

> **Q:** *What is the difference between the Calgary Flames and a bra?*
>
> **A:** *A bra has two cups.*

"Come on, then," he says to the Devil, "have him drop the puck."

"This is hell," says the Devil. "We haven't got any pucks."

Burglars recently broke into the Ottawa Senators home arena and stole the entire contents of the trophy room. Police are looking for a man carrying a carpet.

Dubious Depiction

A lady walks into a tattoo parlour. She's been told that the artist is the best. Being a huge Wayne Gretzky fan, she requests that he put Gretzky's face on her inner thigh. After an hour of work, the artist finishes and shows the lady his work.

> "This is the only country in the world where, in thousands of gardens, tomato plants are held up with broken hockey sticks. This is a unique Canadian happening."
>
> –Robert F. Harney, former director of the Multicultural History Society of Ontario

"This doesn't look anything like Gretzky," she says.

He takes out a picture of Gretzky and compares them. "See, they look just alike."

The lady does not agree and threatens to sue. So the artist agrees to do Gretzky for free on her left thigh. He does the tattoo and excitedly shows it to her.

"This one doesn't look like Wayne Gretzky, either!" she screams.

The artist insists the tattoo is identical to the picture of Gretzky that she brought. To solve the debate, the artist asks his friend, a huge hockey fan, to come by the shop and give his opinion. So the friend comes over, and the lady lifts her dress completely over her head, revealing her tattoos and the fact that she is not wearing panties.

"Hmmmm," says the artist's friend. "I'm not sure who the wingers are, but the centre is definitely Lanny McDonald."

Q: *What is the Meaning of the Toronto Maple LEAFS?*

A: Losers Even After Forty Seasons *(and it works for another decade too! Sorry.)*

Canadians in Saudi Arabia

A Toronto Argonauts fan, an Edmonton Eskimos fan and a Calgary Stampeders fan are in Saudi Arabia performing military duty for the Canadian army.

While off base, they are caught sharing a smuggled case of booze. All of a sudden, Saudi police rush in and arrest them. The mere possession of alcohol is a severe offence in Saudi Arabia, so for their terrible crime, the soldiers are sentenced to death.

With the help of good lawyers, they successfully appeal their death sentence down to life imprisonment. Then, by a stroke of luck, a benevolent sheik decides that they can be released after receiving just 20 lashes of the whip.

"Canada is a country whose main exports are hockey players and cold fronts. Our main imports are baseball players and acid rain."

–Pierre Elliott Trudeau

As they are preparing for their punishment, the sheik says, "It's my first wife's birthday today, and she has asked me to allow each one of you one wish before your whipping."

The Argos fan is first in line because he had the least to drink. He thinks for a while and then says, "Please tie a pillow to my back." The pillow is tied in place, but it lasts only 10 lashes before the whip goes through it. The Argos fan is carried away bleeding and crying.

The Eskimos fan is up next because he consumed almost a quarter of the case by himself. After watching the scene, he says, "Okay, please fix two pillows to my back." But even two pillows can take only 15 lashes before the whip goes through, sending the Eskimos fan off crying like a baby.

Q: *What do the Vancouver Canucks and the* Titanic *have in common?*

A: *They both look good until they hit the ice.*

The Stampeders fan is the last up because he finished off the rest of the crate of liquor (and given his team allegiances, who can blame him?). But before he can say anything, the sheik turns to him and says, "You support the greatest Canadian football team. Your supporters are the best and most loyal fans in all the world. For this you may have two wishes."

> **Q:** *What do a preacher and the Edmonton Eskimos have in common?*
>
> **A:** *They both make people stand up and shout, "Jesus Christ!"*

"Thanks, your most royal highness," the Stampeders fan replies. "In recognition of your kindness, my first wish is that you give me not 20, but 100 lashes."

"Not only are you an honourable and powerful man, you are also very brave," says the sheik. "If 100 lashes is what you desire, then so be it. And your second wish? What is it to be?" the sheik asks.

To which the Stampeders fan replies, "Tie the Eskimos and Argos fans to my back."

Team Passion

A wife is watching the news with her husband when she turns to him and says, "Did you her that? A man in Winnipeg swapped his wife for a season ticket to all the Jets games. Would you do a thing like that?"

"Heck no!" says the husband. "The season is half over."

CFL Press Release

Bowing to political correctness and pressure from First Nations peoples, the Edmonton Eskimos have agreed to change their name. They will now be know as the Edmonton Tampons—a name chosen because the team is good for only one period and doesn't have a second string.

Four hockey fans decide to climb Mount Everest. Each climber just happens to be a huge fan of a different NHL team. They are friends, but when it comes to hockey, they are bitter enemies. As they climb higher and higher, they continually argue about which one of them is most loyal to his team.

Finally, as they reach the summit, the climber from Vancouver takes a running jump off the edge, screams "This is for the Vancouver Canucks!" and plummets to his death.

> I just started watching the Calgary Flames. My doctor said I should avoid excitement.

Not wanting to be outdone, the climber from Ottawa throws himself off the mountain and shouts, "This is for the Ottawa Senators!" He also plummets to his death.

Seeing this, the Montréal climber walks to the edge of the cliff and yells, "This is for all hockey fans!" and pushes the guy from Toronto off the cliff.

Top 25 Reasons Hockey is Better Than Sex

25. It's okay to bleed during play.
24. If it's a bad game, you can call a time out.
23. Every player usually has two or three sticks to choose from.
22. There is a limit to the sizes of all equipment.
21. You can still play when you get married.
20. You can change on the fly.
19. Anytime you see an open net, you can go for it.
18. If you can't get it up, who cares?
17. You can score on all the teams in the league over and over.
16. You can pull the goalie without getting yelled at.
15. It is broadcast live on TV.
14. Everyone can shoot at the same goal.
13. You can shoot into the goal, and it's a good thing.
12. Because of the visor, nothing can get in your eyes.
11. You always know how big the stick is.
10. It's legal to play hockey professionally.
9. The puck is always hard.
8. Protective equipment is reusable, and you don't even have to wash it.
7. It lasts a full hour.
6. You know you're finished when the buzzer sounds.

5. Your parents cheer when you score.
4. When you're tired, you're expected to get off and let a buddy take your place.
3. You can count on it at least twice a week.
2. You can tell your friends about it afterward.

And, the number one reason hockey is better than sex...

1. A two-on-one or three-on-one is not uncommon.

The Seven Dwarves

The Seven Dwarves are trapped in a mineshaft. Snow White runs to the entrance and yells down to them.

From the dark void, a voice calls back, "The Hamilton Tiger-Cats will win the Grey Cup in 2013."

Snow White sighs, "Thank God...at least Dopey's still alive!"

Toronto Maple Leafs general manager Brian Burke and a priest are playing a friendly game of golf. Burke takes his first shot, misses and says, "Jesus, dammit, I missed."

The priest is shocked and warns the foul-mouthed Burke, "Don't use that kind of language, or God will punish you."

On his next shot, Burke misses again and under his breath whispers, "Jesus effing Christ."

Did you hear the Leafs have a new Chinese-born coach? His name is Win Won Soon.

The priest overhears him and says, "My son, please refrain from blasphemy or God will surely punish you."

Burke, never one to censor himself, approaches the ball, takes his shot, misses again and without pause says, "Jesus H. Christ, I missed again."

Suddenly, a bolt of lightning strikes and kills the priest instantly. A voice from the heavens booms forth, "Jesus, missed again...."

The Toronto Raptors are so bad that to prepare the team for the crowd noise they will hear during the season, the coach runs practices with a laugh track.

Mad Manager

The Toronto Raptors manager doesn't stand for any nonsense. When he catches a couple of fans sneaking past security, he is furious.

He grabs them by the collars and says, "Now you just get back in there and watch the game until it finishes."

Q: *What's the difference between the Toronto Maple Leafs and a cigarette vending machine?*

A: The vending machine has Players.

Hotline

The Toronto Maple Leafs have apparently set up a call centre for fans who are troubled by their current form. The number is 1-800-510-10-10. Calls are charged at peak rate for overseas users. Once again, that number is 1-800 five won nothing won nothing won nothing.

> **Q:** *Why was Cinderella thrown off the Toronto Raptors?*
>
> **A:** *Because she kept running away from the ball.*

Toronto sports fans are so dumb that when you ask them what bird symbolizes the Toronto Blue Jays, they can't figure it out.

Say a Little Prayer

At a Montréal Canadiens team-sponsored banquet for its hockey legends, the Bishop of Montréal sits at the head table and is called upon to say grace. A little excited and star struck by some of the great players in the room—such as Jean Béliveau, Maurice Richard and Guy Lafleur—the bishop has a little trouble with the reading.

"Thank you, Lord, for what we are about to eat," he says and then concludes with, "In the name of the Father, the Son and the Goalie Host."

Montréal's Olympic Stadium is widely known in the rest of the world as the "Big O" because of its oval shape, but Montréalers have a different name for it because it has cost them so much to build: "The Big Owe."

A Canadian at the Olympics

An American, a Russian and a Canadian go to Beijing for the 2008 Olympic Summer Games to cheer on their respective countries but quickly find out it is difficult to find tickets for the events, so they have to come up with a sneaky way to get in.

> *Q: What has 82 legs and lives in the cellar?*
>
> *A: The Hamilton Tiger-Cats.*

The American sees a couple of kids playing with a soccer ball and suddenly has a brilliant idea. He takes the ball and approaches the players' entrance. When the guard stops him, he says confidently, "United States, soccer!"

The guard steps aside.

The Russian sees the American's plan work and knows he can do the same. He spots some kids playing basketball and grabs an extra ball. When the guard stops him, he says. "Russia, basketball!"

The guard lets him pass.

The Canadian thinks, "This is easy! No problem." He looks around and sees some barbed wire. He picks it up, takes it to the players' entrance and says, "Canada, fencing!"

Canadian Sports and Society

A study by the Canadian National Sports Society examines the recreational preferences of Canadians from all social and economic levels. Below are the most interesting findings from the study:

The sport of choice for the unemployed or the incarcerated is basketball.

The sport of maintenance and grounds keepers is football.

The sport of the front-line service worker is bowling.

The sport of the supervisor is baseball.

The sport for the middle management type is tennis.

> **Q:** *Why doesn't the NHL want to establish a team in Hamilton?*
>
> **A:** *Because then Toronto would want a new team, too.*

The sport for the upwardly mobile corporate bigwig is golf.

The conclusion of the report: The higher you are on the corporate ladder, the smaller your balls.

To Hell and Back

A man knocks on the Pearly Gates. His face is old, and his clothes are stained. He trembles and shakes with fear as St. Peter speaks, "What have you done to gain admission here?"

"Sir, I've been a loyal Montréal Canadiens fan all my life," says the man.

The Pearly Gates suddenly swung open.

"Come in and choose your harp angel," St. Peter says. "You've had your fair share of hell."

Smart Dog

A man walks into a Montréal bar with a dog. The bartender says, "You can't bring that dog in here."

"You don't understand," says the man. "This is no regular dog. He can talk."

"Listen, pal," says the bartender. "If that dog can talk, I'll give you $100."

The man puts the dog on a stool and asks him, "What's on top of a house?"

"Roof!"

"Right. And what's on the outside of a tree?"

"Bark!"

"And who's the greatest hockey player of all time?"

"Howe!"

"I guess you've heard enough," says the man. "I'll take the $100 in 20s."

The bartender is furious. "Listen, pal," he says, "get out of here before I belt you."

As soon as they're on the street, the dog turns to the man and says, "Do you think I should have said 'Richard?'"

Q: What do the Leafs and the Blue Jays have in common?

A: Neither can play hockey.

Old Timers

Three old hockey fans are in church one Sunday in September, praying for their teams.

The first one asks, "Lord, when will the Oilers win the Stanley Cup again?"

God replies, "In five years."

"But I'll be dead by then," says the man.

> In a survey, four out of five dentists recommend playing hockey.

The second one asks, "Lord, when will the Flames win the Stanley Cup?"

The Lord answers, "In 10 years."

"But I'll be dead by then," says the man.

The third one asks, "Oh Lord, when will the Leafs win the Stanley Cup again?"

God answers, "I'll be dead by then!"

At one point during a game, the coach calls one of his seven-year-old hockey players aside and asks, "Do you understand what cooperation is? What a team is?"

The little boy nods in the affirmative.

"Do you understand that what matters is not whether we win or lose, but how we play together as a team?"

The little boy nods.

"So," the coach continues, "I'm sure you know, when a penalty is called, you shouldn't argue, curse, attack the referee or call him a peckerhead. Do you understand all that?"

> **Q:** *How do you spot a counterfeit hockey ticket?*
>
> **A:** *It contains the word Toronto on it.*

Again the little boy nods.

The coach continues, "And when I call you off the ice so that another boy gets a chance to play, it's not good sportsmanship to call your coach a 'dumb asshole,' right?"

Again the little boy nods.

"Good," says the coach. "Now go over there and explain all that to your mother."

A hockey fan dies and is met at the Pearly Gates by an angel that offers to take him on a tour of Heaven. As they walk the grounds, the hockey fan notices what looks like a hockey rink and asks if he can go inside. The angel, of course, says yes.

> **Q:** *How do you keep the Vancouver Canucks out of your yard?*
>
> **A:** *Put up a goal net.*

Upon entering the rink, the hockey fan is awestruck when he sees a lone skater going up and down the ice. The skater is graceful and fast, and he makes moves that seem impossible for mere mortals. And he has on a Bruins jersey with #4 on the back.

The hockey fan turns to the angel with tears welling up in his eyes and says, "Oh my God, that's Bobby Orr. Did he die?"

The angel's response comes as a relief. "No. That's God, but he thinks he's Bobby Orr."

Moaning

Three Maple Leafs fans are bemoaning the fact that their team keeps losing and might miss the playoffs.

"I blame the manager," says the first fan. "If he would sign new players, we could have a great team."

"I blame the players," says the second fan. "If they made more of an effort, I am sure we would score more goals."

"I blame my parents," adds the third fan. "I'd been born in another city, I'd be supporting a decent team!"

Q: *What do you call a Vancouver Canuck with a Stanley Cup ring?*

A: *A thief.*

Dear Abby,

I have never written to you before, but I really need your advice. I suspect that my wife has been cheating on me. The phone rings but if I answer, the caller hangs up. My wife has been going out with "the girls" a lot recently, but when I ask their names, she always says, "just some friends from work. You don't know them." I try to stay awake and look out for her when she comes home, but I usually fall asleep. Anyway, I have not broached the subject with my wife. I think deep down I just did not want to know the truth, but last night she went out again and I decided to finally check on her. Around midnight, I hid in the garage behind my hockey equipment so I could get a good view of the whole street when she arrived home from a night out with the girls. When she got out of the car, she was buttoning up her blouse, and she took her panties out of her purse and slipped them on. It was at that moment, crouching behind my hockey gear, that I noticed a hairline crack where the blade meets the graphite shaft on my new one-piece hockey stick. Is this something I can fix myself, or should I take it back to the pro-shop where I bought it?

Q: *What do the Vancouver Canucks and possums have in common?*

A: *Both play dead at home and are killed on the road.*

Legends in Heaven

Mario Lemieux, Steve Yzerman and Wayne Gretzky all die and meet in heaven. God is sitting in His chair waiting for them. He says to the three legends, "Gentlemen before I let you in, you must tell me what you believe. Mario we'll start with you. In what do you believe?"

"I believe hockey is the greatest thing in the world and the best sport in history."

To that, God says, "Take the seat to my left." God then turns to Steve and says, "Steven, in what do you believe?"

Steve replies, "I believe to be the best, you've got to give every ounce you've got!"

To that god says, "Take the seat to my right." He then turns to number 99 and says, "Wayne, tell me, what do you believe?"

To which Wayne replies, "I believe you are sitting in my seat."

Play-by-play announcer in a game between the Vancouver Canucks and the Toronto Maple Leafs: "And here comes the Leafs' Grabovski, with a pass to Antropov, then it's to Kulemin. Oh, the Canucks' Hordichuk grabs the puck, then shoots a quick pass to Sedin, over to Bieksa, to the point to Ohlund. It's blocked and picked up by the Leafs, and here comes Blake...Blake? What kind of ridiculous name is Blake for a hockey player?"

My American Wife

Q: How many Vancouver Canucks does it take to win a Stanley Cup?

A: Nobody knows and we may never find out.

As it is in many Canadian homes on New Year's Eve, my wife and I face the annual conflict over what is more important, the World Junior Championship Hockey games on television or New Year's

Eve dinner. To keep the peace, I eat dinner with the rest of the family and even linger for some pleasant after-dinner conversation before retiring to the family room to turn on the game. Several minutes later, my wife comes downstairs and graciously brings a cold drink for me. She smiles, kisses me on the cheek and asks what the score is. I tell her it is the end of the second period and that the score is still nothing to nothing. "See?" she says. "You didn't miss a thing."

> **Q:** *What does a Senators fan do after he wins the Cup?*
>
> **A:** *He turns off the Xbox.*

Sidney Crosby goes into the Pittsburgh changing room to find his teammates looking glum.

"What's up?" he asks.

They reply, "We're having trouble getting motivated for this game—it's only Toronto."

Crosby says: "I think I can beat them by myself—you go to the bar and relax."

So Crosby plays Toronto by himself.

After a few drinks, the rest of the team wonders how the game is going, so they ask the bartender to turn on the TV. The score reads: "Pittsburgh 1, Toronto 0 (Crosby, 10th min, 1st period)." After several more drinks, they check the final score on the TV. It says, "Pittsburgh 1, Toronto 1 (Finger, 19th min, 3rd period)."

They can't believe that Crosby has single-handedly pulled off a tie against Toronto, so they rush to the arena to congratulate him. However, he is sitting with his head in his hands, wailing, "I let you down."

"Don't be silly," they say. "You got a draw against Toronto—and they only scored at the very end."

"No, no," he cries, "I have, I've let you down! Stupid, stupid, stupid! I got sent off after 12 minutes!"

Hockey Players versus Monks

The Edmonton Oilers play an exhibition match against a team from a visiting monastery. Just before the first period, the visiting team—all of whom are monks—kneel solemnly on the ice, put their hands together and indulge in five minutes of silent prayer. The monastery then trounces their hosts 13–1. After the match, the Edmonton captain says, "Well boys, we've been out-played before, but this is the first time we've ever been out-prayed."

> **Q:** *How do you know spring is here?*
>
> **A:** *The Leafs are out.*

Hockey Player Double Entendre

When the Brunette grabs his Peca, she just can't stop Tugnutt. Excitedly, she screams, "Holik cow, your Wiemer is Luongo and Fata. Bonk me now and make it Messier!"

Top 10 Signs There's a Rookie in the Dressing Room

10. He's the only guy in the room who can't grow a playoff beard.
9. He actually follows curfew.
8. He keeps asking, "Can I drive the Zamboni? Can I? Can I, please?"
7. He has Proactiv in his locker.
6. He blushes every time he sees the cheerleaders.
5. He is scared of girls.
4. He can't buy beer for the team.
3. After practice he goes to work at McDonald's.
2. Growing up, he idolized Sidney Crosby.
1. He cries for his mom on road trips.

The Goaltender's Psalm

The puck is my shepherd;
I shall not ice.
It maketh me save in unnatural positions;
It leadeth me into leg splits;
It restoreth my fans' faith;
It leadeth me in the paths of odd-man rushes.
Yea, though I skate in the valley of the shadow of the net,
I will fear no sniper;
For my stick is with me;
My facemask and pads, they comfort me;

I anointeth my body with sports cream;
My back-up tipeth over!
Surely coaches and trainers shall follow me
All the games of my life.
And I shall dwell in the Montréal Forum forever.

> **Q:** *How does Wayne Gretzky stay cool?*
>
> **A:** *He sits next to his fans.*

Chapter Ten

The 49th Parallel

You Don't Say!

Canadians will explain the appeal of curling to Americans if they can explain the appeal of the National Rifle Association to us!

God On the Eighth Day

Everyone knows the story of God creating the world in six days and resting on the seventh...well, on the eighth day, God and the angel Gabriel are looking down on the world and God says to Gabriel, "I am happy with my creation, Gabriel. So happy, in fact, that today I will create the best land in the world, and I will call this land Canada. Oh Gabriel, it will be most beautiful.

> **Q:** *How are American beer and having sex in a rowboat alike?*
>
> **A:** *They are both so close to water!*

"I will give it tall, majestic mountains, and wide-open prairies. I will give it not one, not even two, but three oceans. I will cover this land in rich green forests, deep blue lakes, crystal clear rivers and beautiful wildlife for them to enjoy. I will let them experience all four seasons, and I will populate this land with all different types of people—nothing but the kindest, gentlest most caring people in the world—and they shall be known as Canadians.

These Canadians will be known around the world for their friendliness and compassion for others, and they will be well respected by all. They will rise up in the face of tyranny and help crush evil that threatens the world. They will be intelligent, and use this intelligence for the good of the world..."

> "A Canadian is merely an unarmed American with health care."
>
> –John Wing

God keeps going on like this for a while, and the entire time Gabriel is becoming quite worried so finally he says, "God, I don't mean to question you, but don't you think that you may be giving these Canadians a little too much?"

God looks upon Gabriel and smiles, then says, "Don't worry Gabriel. Wait until you see the neighbours I am giving them!"

A Canadian and an American are having a beer together, and the conversation turns to who has the better country. After numerous exchanges of boasts, the Yankee says, "Sure, Canada's nice! But take away your clean air, your friendly people and your strong beer, and what have you got?"

> "God Bless America, but God help Canada to put up with them!"
>
> –Anonymous

The Canuck smiles and says, "Easy—the United States!"

After the Game

Three Canadians and three Americans are travelling to a hockey game. The three Americans each buy tickets then watch as the three Canadians buy only one.

"How are the three of you going to travel on only one ticket?" asks an American.

"Watch and you'll see," says one Canadian.

They all board the train. The Americans take their respective seats, but all three Canadians cram into a bathroom and close the door behind them.

Shortly after the train has departed, the conductor comes around collecting tickets. He knocks on the bathroom door and says, "Ticket, please!" The door opens a crack, and a single arm emerges with a ticket in hand. The conductor takes it and moves on. The Americans see this and agree that it is brilliant.

So after the game, they decide to copy the Canadians on the return trip and save some money. When they get to the station, they buy a single ticket for their return trip. To their astonishment, the Canadians don't buy a ticket at all.

> "I get to go to lots of overseas places, like Canada."
>
> –Britney Spears, when asked the best part of being famous.

"How are you going to travel with no ticket?" asks one of the confused Americans.

"Watch and you'll see," reply the Canadians.

When they board the train, the three Americans cram into a bathroom, and the three Canadians cram into another bathroom nearby.

Once the train leaves the station, one of the Canadians exits the bathroom and walks over to the other bathroom where the Americans are hiding, knocks on the door and says, "Ticket, please!"

An American man calls home to his wife and says, "Honey I have been asked to go fishing at a big lake up in Canada with my boss and several of his friends. We'll be gone for a week. This is a good opportunity for me to get that promotion I've been wanting, so would you please pack me enough clothes for a week and set out my rod and tackle box? We're leaving from the office, and I will swing by the house to pick my things up. Oh! Please pack my new blue silk pajamas."

> "It is a peaceful, nice country with lots of empty space, a boring government that never faces serious crises, a minimal trade partner and the source of singers with strange accents."
>
> –John Dickinson

The wife thinks this sounds a little fishy, but being a good wife she does exactly what her husband asks.

The following weekend, he comes home a little tired but otherwise looking good. The wife welcomes him home and asks if he caught many fish.

He says, "Yes! Lots of walleye, some bluegill and a few pike. But why didn't you pack my new blue silk panamas like I asked you to do?"

"I did. They're in your tackle box."

A Canadian is drinking in a New York bar when he gets a call on his cell phone. He hangs up, grinning from ear to ear, and orders a round of drinks for everybody in the bar because, he announces, his wife has just given birth to a typical Canadian baby boy weighing 11 kilograms.

> "Canada has always been the world's largest per capita consumer of Kraft Dinner, and despite its American origins, the product has become a part of Canadian culture."
>
> –Author Unknown

Nobody can believe that any new baby can weigh 11 kilos, but the Canuck just shrugs.

"That's about average up north, folks. Like I said, my boy's a typical Canadian baby boy." Congratulations shower him from all around, and many exclamations of "WOW" are heard. One woman actually faints because of sympathy pains.

Two weeks later, the Canadian returns to the bar. The bartender says, "Say, you're the father of that typical Canadian baby that weighed 11 kilograms at birth, aren't you? Everybody's been making' bets about how big he'd be in two weeks.

We were gonna call you...so how much does he weigh now?"

The proud father answers, "Almost 8 kilos." The bartender is puzzled and concerned.

"What happened? He already weighed 11 kilograms the day he was born."

The Canadian father takes a slow swig from his Molson beer, wipes his lips on his shirt sleeve, leans into the bartender and proudly says, "Had him circumcised."

Distance

An American blond calls the airline and asks, "Can you tell me how long it'll take to fly from Seattle to Montréal?"

The agent replies, "Just a minute..."

"Thank you," the blonde says and hangs up.

An avid Canadian fisherman decides to cross the Peace Bridge to Lewiston and fish the American side of the Niagara River.

He settles down on a quiet dock and begins to fill his bucket with some nice fish when an American game warden approaches him and says, "May I see your fishing licence please?"

> "The US is our trading partner, our neighbour, our ally and our friend... and sometimes we'd like to give them such a smack!"
>
> –Rick Mercer

When he hands over his licence, the game warden laughs and says that it is no good because it is a Canadian fishing licence.

At this point the fisherman replies, "But I'm only catching Canadian fish."

The warden scratches his head for a moment and finally asks, "What do you mean?"

The fisherman reaches in his bucket and pulls out a fish and asks the warden, "What kind of fish is that?"

The warden looks and says, "It's a smallmouth bass."

The fisherman replies, "See what I mean. If it was an American fish, it would be a largemouth bass."

An American decides to write a book about famous churches around the world. For his first chapter, he decides to write about American churches. So he buys a plane ticket and takes a trip to Orlando, thinking that he will work his way across the country from south to north.

On his first day, he is inside a church taking photographs when he notices a golden telephone mounted on the wall with a sign that reads: $10,000 per call.

The American is intrigued and asks a priest who is strolling by what the telephone is used for. The priest replies that it is a direct line to heaven, and that for

$10,000 you can talk to God. The American thanks the priest and goes on his way.

> "I don't even know what street Canada is on."
>
> –Al Capone

His next stop is in Atlanta. There, at a very large cathedral, he sees the same golden telephone with the same sign under it. He wonders if this is the same kind of telephone he saw in Orlando, and he asks a nearby nun what its purpose is. She tells him that it is a direct line to heaven, and that for $10,000 he can talk to God.

"Okay, thank you," says the American. He then travels to Indianapolis, Washington D.C., Philadelphia, Boston and New York. In every church, he sees the same golden telephone with the same sign under it.

The American, upon leaving Vermont, sees a sign for Canada and decides to see if Canadians have the same phone. He arrives in Ottawa, and again, there is the same golden telephone, but this time the sign under it reads: 50 cents per call. The American is surprised, so he asks the priest about the sign. "Father, I've travelled all over America, and I've seen this same golden telephone in many churches. I'm told that it is a direct line to heaven, but in every state the price was $10,000 per call. Why is it so cheap here?"

The priest smiles and answers, "You're in Canada now, son. It's a local call."

U.S. Navy versus Canada

This is the transcript of the actual radio conversation between a U.S. naval ship and the Canadian authorities off the coast of Newfoundland, October 1995. Radio conversation released by the Chief of Naval Operations 10-10-95.

Canadians: Please divert your course 15 degrees to the south to avoid a collision.

Americans: Recommend you divert your course 15 degrees to the north.

Canadians: Negative. You will have to divert your course 15 degrees to the south to avoid a collision.

Americans: This is the Captain of a U.S. Navy ship. I say again, divert *your* course.

Canadians: No. I say again, you divert *your* course.

Americans: This is the aircraft carrier USS *Lincoln*, the second largest ship in the United States Atlantic fleet. We are accompanied by three destroyers, three cruisers and numerous support vessels. I demand that you change your course 15 degrees north, I say again, that's one five degrees north, or counter measures will be undertaken to ensure the safety of this ship.

Canadians: We are a lighthouse. Your call.

This is a true story...

An elderly Canadian lady living in Florida does her shopping and, upon returning to her car, finds four males in the act of stealing her vehicle. She drops her shopping bags and draws her handgun, screaming at the top of her voice, "I have a gun, and I know how to use it! Get out of the car!"

The four men don't wait for a second invitation. They get out and run like mad. The lady, somewhat shaken, then loads her shopping bags into the back of the car and gets into driver's seat. She is so flustered that she can't get her key into the ignition.

> "I've been to Canada, and I've always gotten the impression that I could take the country over in about two days."
>
> –Jon Stewart

She tries and tries, and then it dawns on her what the problem must be. A few minutes later, she finds *her* car parked four or five spaces farther down. She loads her bags into the car and drives to the police station.

The sergeant to whom she tells the story can't stop laughing. He points to the other end of the counter, where four pale men are reporting a car jacking by a mad, elderly woman described as white, less than 5 feet tall, glasses, curly white hair, and carrying a large handgun.

No charges are filed.

If you're going to have a senior moment, make it a memorable one!

Rednecks in Canada

Two good old boys from Alabama who love to fish want to do some of that ice fishing they've heard so much about, so they take a trip to Canada to give it a try.

> "Canada could have enjoyed English government, French culture and American know-how. Instead, it wound up with English know-how, French government and American culture."
>
> –Author/anthropologist J. R. Colombo

The lake is nicely frozen, so they stop and get all their tackle at a little bait shop near the lake.

One of them says, "We're going to need an ice pick."

After they get their equipment, they take off. In about two hours, one of them is back at the shop and says, "We're going to need another dozen ice picks."

The shop owner sells him the picks, and the good old boy leaves.

In about an hour, he is back at the shop and says, "We're going to need all the ice picks you've got."

The bait man can't stand it any longer. "By the way," he asks, "how are you fellows doing?"

"Not very well at all," he says. "We don't even have the stupid boat in the water yet."

Chapter Eleven
Funny Canadian Facts

What's in a Name

The letter "Z" comes from the Greek letter zeta and should be pronounced *zed* not *zee.* Americans pronounce it *zee* to make the alphabet song rhyme. Somebody tell Jay-Zed.

PEI Pull

Actor Charles Francis Coghlan was born in Paris, France, but moved to North America and fell in love with a little piece of land in Fortune Bridge, Prince Edward Island. Although he spent most of his time on the road as part of an acting troupe, he purchased a charming little farm in Fortune Bridge to be his summer and retirement home.

Unfortunately, Coghlan never got to enjoy that piece of land as he died in 1899 of an unknown illness while in Galveston, Texas. He was buried in a lead-lined coffin. Less than a year later, a devastating hurricane blew through the Gulf of Mexico, bringing widespread flooding that washed Coghlan's coffin out to sea. His acting club offered a reward for the coffin's return for several years, but

> "The great themes of Canadian history are as follows: Keeping the Americans out, keeping the French in and trying to get the Natives to somehow disappear."
>
> –Will Ferguson

after more seven years passed, his family and friends had given up hope of ever finding him.

Then in 1908, off the coast of PEI, fishermen pulled a barnacle-encrusted coffin out of the Gulf of St. Lawrence close to that piece of farmland Coghlan had purchased as his retirement property. Coghlan hitched a ride on the Gulf Stream and finally got to enjoy his retirement home.

Nova Scotians, like it or not, have long been known as Canada's Bluenoses, but the origin of the name has been lost to time. Some say it was based on a local variety of potato called the "Irish bluenose potato." Others claim it comes from badly dyed fishermen's gloves that left people's faces dyed blue whenever they touched themselves.

People from Halifax are called Haligonians.

Anne of Green Gables

Every year, thousands of tourists flock to Prince Edward Island to visit the home of the iconic Anne Shirley as written in Lucy Maud Montgomery's book *Anne of Green Gables.* You can tour the Green Gables Farm in Cavendish, PEI, and even walk through a replica of Avonlea Town. The books were made even more popular by the CBC series of the same name. But if you want to see the house that was used in that show, you will have to go to the outskirts of Toronto.

The Infamous Loonie

When it was first announced that the Royal Canadian Mint was going to replace the $1 bill with a coin, many Canadians were none too pleased about the change (pun intended). But when the coin was introduced and Canadians saw the iconic loon stamped into the gold-coloured coin, we embraced the change and quickly made it part of our culture. This replacement coin was dubbed the "loonie," and we rejoiced in the silliness of its name. The loonie became more than just a unit of currency when, after Canada won gold in hockey at the 2002 Winter Olympics in Salt Lake City, the Canadian ice technician revealed that he had embedded a lucky loonie in the ice to help the team win their first Winter Olympic hockey gold in 50 years! After that, the loonie became a national symbol. That symbol, however, was almost something completely different.

> "Canadian money is also called the loonie. How can you take an economic crisis seriously?"
>
> –Robin Williams

After months of tinkering with a design, the Royal Canadian Mint had originally decided that the new dollar coin would bear a similar design to our old silver dollar, which featured two guys paddling in a canoe. The Royal Canadian Mint called a courier service to take the master stamp from Ottawa to the production plant in Winnipeg. Some guy showed up to pick up the package, signed the papers and left with the one-of-a-kind stamp. Well, that guy disappeared with the stamp, leaving the Royal Canadian Mint in a bit of a quandary. With the date of the big reveal looming, a complete redesign was out of the question, and they could not run the risk of using the same design (which is what the thief was hoping they would do) so the mint had to pull out a secondary design, which just so happened to be a loon. We must thank the unknown thief, for without him, we might be spending canoeies instead.

> "Canada is the only country in the world that knows how to live without an identity."
>
> –Marshall McLuhan

Unique Canadian Words and Their Meanings

Toque: a piece of clothing we could not live without—many thanks to the *coureur des bois*!

Two-four (pronounced *two-fur*): 24 case of beer.

Hockey: you all know what it means, but it is a Canadian word and it is OUR SPORT!

Hoser: popularized by the characters Bob and Doug McKenzie from the SCTV sketches and the movie *Strange Brew,* the word "hoser" describes a particular type of Canadian. A hoser is someone who is slow, oafish, most likely drinking a beer, wearing a plaid jacket and a toque. Although it was originally meant as a derogatory remark, some Canadians have come to embrace it and now use it as a term of endearment.

Sashay: although the drag queen RuPaul popularized the term sashay in his 1993 hit song "Supermodel (You Better Work)," the word is actually Canadian. It comes from a dance performed by French explorers in the early life of the country. It is a gliding dance step used in both ballet and square dancing. Informally, the term was used to insult a male dancer who moved with an effeminate stride.

Homo milk: better known as homogenized milk, it is milk with a fat content of 3.5 percent. Milk cartons emblazoned with the words "homo milk" sometimes make tourists (Americans) laugh, but for us Canadians it is completely normal to be at a friend's house and ask for some homo milk without anyone bursting out in giggles.

Screech: a particularly strong brand of rum from Newfoundland, screech got its name during World War II. Newfoundland was the home of several U.S. bases, and one evening a bored American serviceman went out for a drink and was tempted into trying a few shots of the rum the locals were downing in great quantities. Well, the American soldier apparently overestimated his tolerance and after just one shot, he let out such a scream that people came running from homes and from the base to see what was wrong. An American sergeant burst into the bar and demanded to know what could have made such a "horrible screech."

One quick Newfoundlander stepped and said, "The screech? Why that was the rum." Since then, the drink has been known as Newfoundland Screech. However, the screech you buy today is nothing like the fire of old. Once regulations and governments got involved, screech lost its potency.

Poutine: the greatest greasy food in the world, hands down, this mix of lumpy cheese curds, greasy fries and thick brown gravy originated in Québec in the late 1950s. Although many towns claim to be the originators of poutine, the most common story is that of restaurateur Frederic Lachance of Warwick, Québec, who created the dish to satisfy a customer's craving for fries and cheese curd. He later added the gravy to the mixture, and the iconic poutine was complete.

Boxer George Chuvalo

One of the greatest boxers of his time, George Chuvalo held the Canadian and Commonwealth heavyweight titles. He fought most of the great heavyweights of his time, including Muhammad Ali...and was never knocked out!

As a young man he was somewhat less formidable. Thankfully, he still had the mind of a professional. One day in his youth, it seems he was taking a stroll along the beach in the Toronto area when he was suddenly confronted by a dozen street kids, who beat him up and stole his wallet. He walked home with two black eyes, puffy cheeks and a torn shirt.

His mother took one look at him and asked, "What happened to you?"

George explained that he had been attacked by a gang of street kids.

Confused, his mother asked, "Why didn't you fight back? You surely could have knocked the hell out of those kids!"

"Sure," replied young George, unashamed. "But my fee at the local boxing club for flooring a champion is $50. I don't fight for free."

—Source *Penguin Book of More Canadian Jokes*

Watch Out for the East German Women with Moustaches

Canadian women did fairly well at the 1976 Summer Olympics in Montréal, with the star of the women's swim team, Nancy Garapick, taking home seven medals, a silver and six bronze, but things could have gone a lot better.

Led by Kornelia Ender, the most muscled 17-year old at the games and possibly on the planet, the East German women were the juggernauts of the swimming events, winning 9 of the 11 gold medals available. To all the other competitors, it was obvious that these women were using performance-enhancing drugs, but the inadequate testing at the Montréal Games was easy to get around.

"Canadians are the people who learned to live without the bold accents of the natural ego-trippers of other lands."

–Marshall McLuhan

Although it was obvious to everyone at the Games, it was only in 1991 after the fall of the Berlin Wall that former East German officials came forward and admitted to a state-sponsored steroid program. Apparently the East German government had sponsored the program for its athletes to prove to the Western powers that East Germany and communism were superior. For athletes like the mini-hulk Ender, blame was placed directly on the "medical men" that gave her the shots they said would help her "regenerate and recuperate." She recalled having been shocked at her 9-kilogram weight gain right before the Games but simply attributed it to hard work. It's hard to believe that she had no idea of the program, but her achievements remain in the record books because the International Olympic Committee cannot overturn results without physical proof of wrongdoing. She remains in the books but with an asterisk.

> "After all, we fought the Yanks in 1812 and kicked them the hell out of our country–but not with blanks."
>
> –Farley Mowat

In the eyes of Canadians, Nancy Garapick and all the rest of the Canadian women's swim team are the true gold-medal winners.

Paul Fortier & David MacLennan

David and Paul have been partners in crime since grade school, when they discovered that their favourite activity was playing jokes on the teacher, the janitor, the principal and all their friends (and each other). Once when the teacher was out of the room, they enlisted the class to help them completely reverse everything in the classroom, including desks, chairs, tables, bulletin boards...anything that wasn't nailed down. The teacher was less than impressed. Since then, whenever they hear about a hilarious or off-colour joke or some crazy prank, they will email each other because they can't help but share it. David definitely wanted Paul's input on this book to get a Québecois' view of the rest of Canada!